CW00418480

The Sorrow

Dulce et decorum est Pro patria mori

Perhaps some day the sun will shine again,
And I shall see that still the skies are blue,
And feel once more I do not live in vain,
Although bereft of You.

Perhaps, by Vera Brittain

THE LINNET'S WINGS

My Boy Jack

"Have you news of my boy Jack?"
Not this tide.
"When d'you think that he'll come back?"
Not with this wind blowing, and this tide.

"Has any one else had word of him?"
Not this tide.
For what is sunk will hardly swim,
Not with this wind blowing, and this tide.

"Oh, dear, what comfort can I find?"
None this tide,
Nor any tide,
Except he did not shame his kind —
Not even with that wind blowing, and that tide.

Then hold your head up all the more,
This tide,
And every tide;
Because he was the son you bore,
And gave to that wind blowing and that tide!

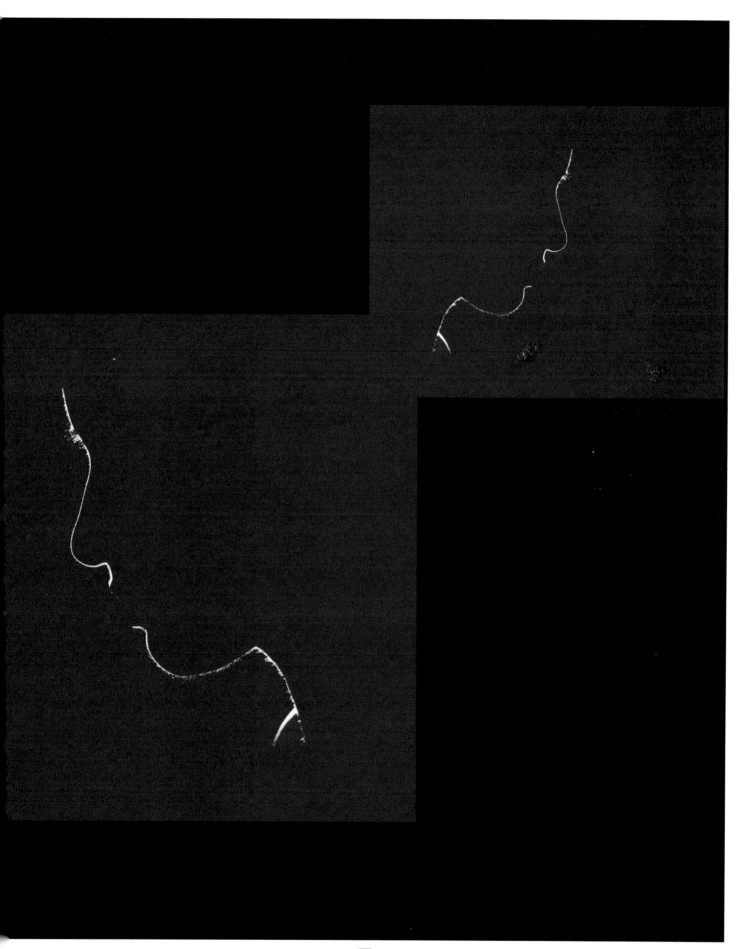

"You can say anything you want, yessir, but it's the words that sing, they soar and descend...I bow to them...I love them, I cling to them, I run them down, I bite into them, I melt them down...I love words so much...The unexpected ones...The ones I wait for greedily or stalk until, suddenly, they drop..."   -- Pablo Neruda

Only On Amazon India

Second Editions:
Blackbird Dock
Purple Kisses

Announcer
El Lissitzky

The total number of military and civilian casualties in World War I was more than 41 million: there were over 18 million deaths and 23 million wounded, ranking it among the deadliest conflicts in human history.

Here Dead We Lie
by A. E. Housman

Here dead we lie
Because we did not choose
To live and shame the land
From which we sprung.

Life, to be sure,
Is nothing much to lose,
But young men think it is,
And we were young.

To Germany
by Charles Hamilton Sorley

You are blind like us. Your hurt no man designed,
And no man claimed the conquest of your land.
But gropers both through fields of thought confined
We stumble and we do not understand.
You only saw your future bigly planned,
And we, the tapering paths of our own mind,
And in each others dearest ways we stand,
And hiss and hate. And the blind fight the blind.

When it is peace, then we may view again
With new won eyes each other's truer form
And wonder. Grown more loving kind and warm
We'll grasp firm hands and laugh at the old pain,
When it is peace. But until peace, the storm,
The darkness and the thunder and the rain.

CLASSIC WIZARDRY

Autumn Fires

In the other gardens
    And all up in the vale,
From the autumn bonfires
    See the smoke trail!

Pleasant summer over,
    And all the summer flowers,
The red fire blazes,
    The grey smoke towers.

Sing a song of seasons!
    Something bright in all!
Flowers in the summer,
    Fires in the fall!

    Robert Louis Stevenson

Dust

This quiet Dust was Gentlemen and Ladies
    And lads and girls;
Was laughter and ability and sighing,
    And frocks and curls;

This passive place a summer's nimble mansion,
    Where bloom and bees
Fulfilled their oriental circuit,
    Then ceased like these.

    Emily Dickinson

Collision and Convergence in Truth, Beauty and Love

LIVE IN PROSE

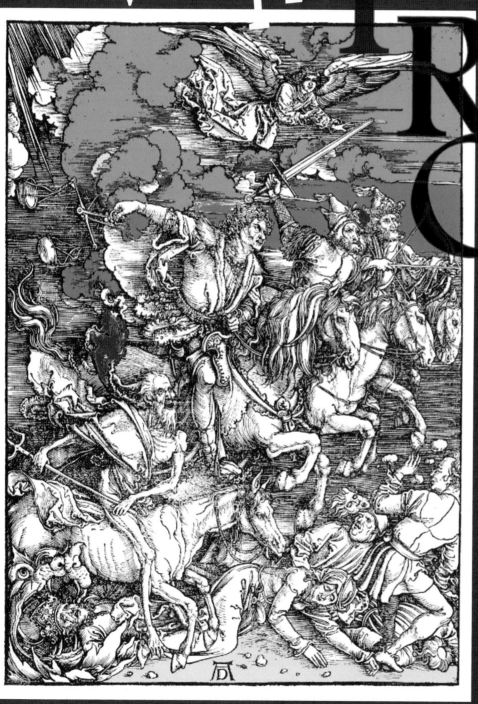

DEATH, FAMINE, PESTILENCE AND WAR: THE FOUR HORSEMEN OF THE APOCALYPSE, BY ALBRECHT DURER, DATE:1498

READ MORE

CONTEMPORARY POETRY, PROSE

AND TRANSLATION

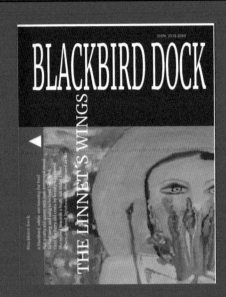

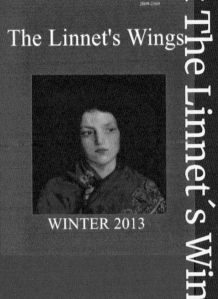

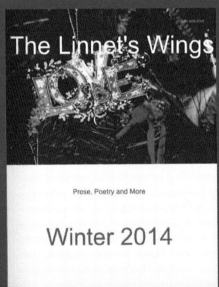

At The Linnet's Wings

Available on Amazon.UK and Amazon.COM

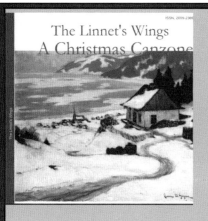

The Linnet's Wings
A Christmas Canzonet

The Linnet's Wings
POETS
Ghosts

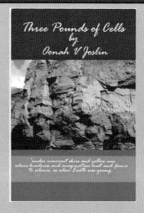

Three Pounds of Cells
by
Oonah V Joslin

Chante Ishta
The Linnet's Wings

There's Magic in the Pictures
The Linnet's Wings
POETS

DISABLED MONSTERS
by
John C. Mannone

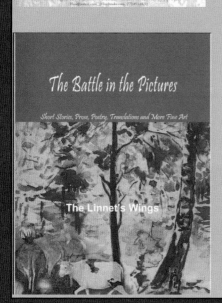

A Christmas Canzonet
The Linnet's Wings
Dreamers

THE GUY THING
BRUCE HARRIS

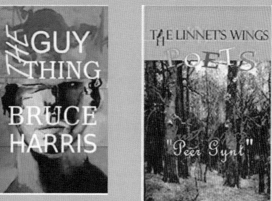

THE LINNET'S WINGS
POETS
"Peer Gynt"

The Battle in the Pictures

Short Stories, Prose, Poetry, Translations and More Fine Art

The Linnet's Wings

The Linnet's Wings

Ghosts

Just Like
"Peer Gynt"

The Linnet's Wings

ME GUSTA

"The Linnet´s Wings Contributors"

Prose, Poetry, Essay and More Fine Art

"gothelinnetswings!"

By 1914, the European powers were divided into two coalitions: the Triple Entente, consisting of France, Russia and Britain and the Triple Alliance of Germany, Austria-Hungary and Italy. The Triple Alliance was primarily defensive in nature, allowing Italy to stay out of the war in 1914, while many of the terms of both agreements were informal and contradicted by others; for example, Italy renewed the Triple Alliance in 1902 but secretly agreed with France to remain neutral if it was attacked by Germany. As the war widened, the Entente added Italy, Japan and eventually the United States to form the Allied Powers, while the Ottoman Empire and Bulgaria joined Germany and Austria to create the Central Powers.

I was always embarrassed by the words sacred, glorious, and sacrifice and the expression in vain. We heard them, sometimes standing in the rain almost out of earshot, so that only the shouted words came through, and had read them, on proclamations that were slapped up by billposters over other proclamations, now for a long time, and I had seen nothing sacred, and the things that were glorious had no glory and the sacrifices were like the dockyards at Chicago if nothing was done with the meat except bury it. There were many words that you could not stand to hear and finally only the names of places had dignity . . . Abstract words such as glory, honour, courage, or hallow were obscene.

Ernest Hemingway

Quoted by Peter Vansittart, Voices of World War One, p248.

"We all want progress, but if you're on the wrong road, progress means doing an about-turn and walking back to the right road; in that case, the man who turns back soonest is the most progressive."

C. S. Lewis

All rights reserved

No part of this publication may be reproduced, distributed, or transmitted in any form or by any means, including photocopying, recording, or other electronic or mechanical methods, without the prior written permission of the publisher, except in the case of brief quotations embodied in critical reviews and certain other noncommercial uses permitted by copyright law. For permission requests, mail the publisher at thelinnetswings@gmail.com

ISBN-13: 978-1727746358

Fall 2018

First Edition

10 /2018

Frontispiece: My Boy Jack by Rudyard Kipling

Other Publication

"The Song of Hiawatha" by Henry Wadsworth Longfellow ISBN 13: 978-1480176423-
-https://www.amazon.com/Song-Hiawatha-Henry-Wadsworth-Longfellow/dp/1480176427
"The House that Jack Built" ISBN-13: 978-1483977669

Chapbooks

"One Day Tells Its Tale to Another" by Nonnie Augustine ISBN-13: 978-1480186354
https://www.amazon.com/One-Day-Tells-Tale-Another/dp/1482730995
"About the Weather-- Spring Trending" by Marie Lynam Fitzpatrick ISBN-13: 978-0993049330
"Disabled Monsters" by John C. Mannone ISBN-13:978-1522869504
https://www.amazon.com/Disabled-Monsters-John-C-Mannone/dp/0993049389
"Three Pounds of Cells" by Oonah V Joslin ISBN-13: 978-0993049378
https://www.amazon.com/Three-Pounds-Cells-Oonah-Joslin/dp/0993049370

Poetry and Photography

"This Crazy Urge to Live" by Bobby Steve Baker ISBN-13: 978-099304909

Short Story Collections

"The Guy Thing" by Bruce Harris ISBN-13: 978-1981116409
https://www.amazon.com/Guy-Thing-Bruce-Harris/dp/1981116400

Poetry Series
Contributors´ Quarterly

Spring Poetry, 2015 ISBN-13: 978-1512051225
https://www.amazon.com/Linnets-Wings-Spring-Poetry-2015/dp/1512051225
Spring Poetry, "Ghosts," 2016 ISBN-13: 978-1517567637
https://www.amazon.com/Linnets-Wings-Poets-Ghosts-Poet/dp/1517567637
Autumn Poets, 2015, ISBN-13: 978-1519157827
https://www.amazon.com/Linnets-Wings-Autumn-Poets-2015/dp/1519157827
Autumn Poets,"There´s Magic in the Pictures" 2016 ISBN-13: 978-1537361659
https://www.amazon.es/Theres-Magic-Pictures-Linnets-Wings/dp/1537361651
Summer Poets, 2015 ISBN-13: 978-1514761717
https://www.amazon.com/Linnets-Wings-Summer-Poets/dp/1514761718
Summer Poets, Just Like "Peer Gynt" ISBN-13: 978-1532865114
https://www.amazon.com/Linnets-Wings-Poets-Just-Like/dp/1533245886

Christmas Series

The Linnet´s Wings: "A Christmas Canzonet" ISBN-13: 978-1519581686
https://www.amazon.com/Linnets-Wings-Christmas-Canzonet/dp/1519581688
The Linnet´s Wings: "A Christmas Canzonet" ISBN-13: 978-1540454935
https://www.amazon.com/Linnets-Wings-Christmas-Canzanet/dp/1540454932
A Christmas Canzonet: "Dreamers" ISBN-13: 978-1977809070
https://www.amazon.com/Christmas-Canzonet-Dreamers-See-Contributors/dp/1977809073

Poem on the Wind: Art and Poetry Series

"Purple Kisses" by Priya Prithviraj ISBN-13: 978-1978203266

Table of Contents

Photoshop

--

Editors:

MANAGING
Marie Lynam Fitzpatrick

SENIOR EDITOR
Bill West

POETRY EDITOR
Oonah Joslin

WEB AND DATABASE DESIGN
Peter Gilkes

Offices

Surface,
Publishing, Corkaree, Mullingar, Co Westmeath, ROI

Design, Carchuna, Granada, Andalucia

Online
The Linnet´s Wings Submissions

Website: www.thelinnetswings.org

"But, first, remember, remember, remember the signs. Say them to yourself when you wake in the morning and when you lie down at night, and when you wake in the middle of the night. And whatever strange things may happen to you, let nothing turn your mind from following the signs. And secondly, I give you a warning. Here on the mountain I have spoken to you clearly: I will not often do so down in Narnia. Here on the mountain, the air is clear and your mind is clear; as you drop down into Narnia, the air will thicken. Take great care that it does not confuse your mind. And the signs which you have learned here will not look at all as you expect them to look, when you meet them there. That is why it is so important to know them by heart and pay no attention to appearances. Remember the signs and believe the signs. Nothing else matters."

C.S. Lewis, The Chronicles of Narnia

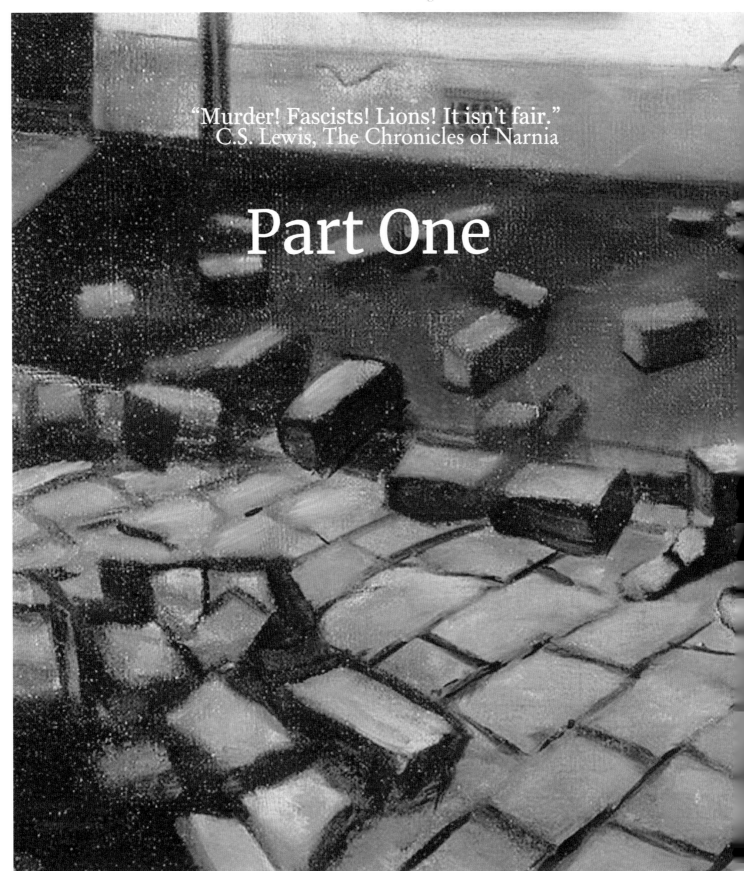

"Murder! Fascists! Lions! It isn't fair."
C.S. Lewis, The Chronicles of Narnia

Part One

A Taube by Christopher Richard Wynne Nevinson--
British paramedic and painter

"The body of a small French schoolboy lies on the
pavement outside a house. The corpse is
surrounded by broken cobblestones from a hole
blown in the street during an air raid."

Date: 1916 (First World War)

"I am the enemy you killed, my friend." Wilfred Owen

Wilfred Owen

by

Bill West

I never met my paternal grandfather, he died long before I was born. I would like to have met him; maybe asked him about his World War I experiences but I doubt he would have told me. Even my father would not talk about World War II until later life because old soldiers never shared their memories of what war was like back then.

I read the War Poets widely, but one writer stood out for me. A soldier who was born the same year as my grandfather, attained the same rank in the army as he did and trained as an officer with the Artists Rifles, though not the same year as my grandfather was there. Perhaps, I thought, I would learn some sense of what the Great War was like, the ugly truths rather than being lulled by patriotic propaganda of the time, to share something of what my grandfather may also have experienced.

Dulce et decorum est pro patria mori which is taken from the Roman poet Horace and means "it is sweet and honourable to die for one's country".

The Shropshire poet, Wilfred Owen died on the 4th November 1918 while attempting to lead his men across the Sambre canal at Ors in France. He died just one week before the Armistice of 11 November 1918. He was 25 years of age.

Born in Oswestry, he grew up in Shrewsbury, Shropshire and appears to have had an enjoyable childhood, exploring the local countryside and visiting local antiquities, the many abbeys and study relics at the ancient Roman ruins near Wroxeter. Sometime in 1913 he wrote Uriconium An Ode, one of two lyric poems (The Swift). Significantly, Uriconium was destroyed by war, a buried sin.

Between January 1917 and November 1918 Wilfred Owen wrote the eight poems for which he is mainly remembered, a more mature poetry than his previous work full of unsettling realism.

THE SENTRY (January 1917)
EXPOSURE (February 1917)
DULCE ET DECORUM EST (August 1917)
ANTHEM FOR DOOMED YOUTH (September 1917)
INSENSIBILITY (November 1917)
FUTILITY (May 1918)
THE SEND-OFF (May 1918)
STRANGE MEETING (September 1918)

In May 1917, whilst being treated for shell-shock at Craiglockhart hospital near Edinburgh, Owen met fellow poet Siegfried Sassoon. Sassoon, a published poet, had been awarded the Military Cross for bravery the previous year but he had developed a strong antipathy towards the conduct of the war. He had written to his commanding officer refusing to return to the front on behalf of all soldiers who were being sacrificed for what he believed were political rather than moral reasons. Sassoon became a poetic mentor to Owen placing great emphasis on "writing from experience" to create the utmost level of realism. In Owen's first drafts of his poem Dulce et decorum est Sassoon's influence can be seen.

Dulce et decorum est refers to the inscription on the chapel wall of the Royal Military College, Sandhurst, Dulce et decorum est pro patria mori which is taken from the Roman poet Horace and means "it is sweet and honourable to die for one's country". Owen's poem describes the effects of a chlorine gas attack on a soldier who was unable reach his gas mask in time. The images and language are the antithesis of 'sweetness' and concepts of 'honour':

Dulce et decorum est

Bent double, like old beggars under sacks,
Knock-kneed, coughing like hags, we cursed through sludge,
Till on the haunting flares we turned out backs,
And towards our distant rest began to trudge.
Men marched asleep. Many had lost their boots,
But limped on, blood-shod. All went lame, all blind;
Drunk with fatigue; deaf even to the hoots
Of gas-shells dropping softly behind.

Gas! GAS! Quick, boys! - An ecstasy of fumbling
Fitting the clumsy helmets just in time,
But someone still was yelling out and stumbling
And flound'ring like a man in fire or lime.-
Dim through the misty panes and thick green light,
As under a green sea, I saw him drowning.

In all my dreams before my helpless sight
He plunges at me, guttering, choking, drowning.

If in some smothering dreams, you too could pace
Behind the wagon that we flung him in,
And watch the white eyes writhing in his face,
His hanging face, like a devil's sick of sin,
If you could hear, at every jolt, the blood
Come gargling from the froth-corrupted lungs
Obscene as cancer, bitter as the cud
Of vile, incurable sores on innocent tongues,-
My friend, you would not tell with such high zest
To children ardent for some desperate glory,
The old Lie: Dulce et decorum est
Pro patria mori.

The old lie is of course the lie that enables the war to continue and keep the British public in ignorance of what was really happening:

My friend, you would not tell with such high zest
To children ardent for some desperate glory,
The old Lie: Dulce et decorum est
Pro patria mori.

Contrary to what some have asserted, Owen was not a bitter, jaundiced pacifist. poet excusing his own fear. He believed in the cessation of the war, but he held to his 'duty.' He had already experienced terrifying events, when he was trapped for days on a railway embankment taking shelter from German artillery fire, lying on the ground surrounded by the remains of a popular fellow officer. This led to the shell-shock that he was being treated for Craiglockhart hospital.

His doctor, Arthur Brock, encouraged Owen in his writing for therapeutic reasons and this approach paid off. Against the advice of Sassoon, although possibly inspired by Sassoon's own example of bravery in the field of battle, Owen requested discharge from hospital to return to the front. Sassoon urged him to accept a medical discharge instead.

In October 1918 he led a unit of his men to storm several enemy positions at Joncourt and for his courage and leadership he was awarded the Military Cross.

Owen said, 'My subject is war, and the pity of war.

Anthem for Doomed Youth

What passing-bells for these who die as cattle?
Only the monstrous anger of the guns.
Only the stuttering rifles' rapid rattle
Can patter out their hasty orisons.
No mockeries now for them; no prayers nor bells;
Nor any voice of mourning save the choirs,
The shrill, demented choirs of wailing shells;
And bugles calling for them from sad shires.

What candles may be held to speed them all?
Not in the hands of boys, but in their eyes
Shall shine the holy glimmers of good-byes.
The pallor of girls' brows shall be their pall;
Their flowers the tenderness of patient minds,
And each slow dusk a drawing-down of blinds.

It was Sassoon who suggested the title of this poem. The suggestion of an anthem, and "shrill, demented choirs of wailing shells" and Owen's use of harsh sounds and onomatopoeic words; "stuttering" and "wailing" and the alliteration of "rifles' rapid rattle" all create a ghastly vision of dehumanisation, of men slaughtered like cattle underlines his lived experience, the pity of war.

29

Strange Meeting
BY WILFRED OWEN

It seemed that out of battle I escaped
Down some profound dull tunnel, long since scooped
Through granites which titanic wars had groined.

Yet also there encumbered sleepers groaned,
Too fast in thought or death to be bestirred.
Then, as I probed them, one sprang up, and stared
With piteous recognition in fixed eyes,
Lifting distressful hands, as if to bless.
And by his smile, I knew that sullen hall,—
By his dead smile I knew we stood in Hell.

With a thousand fears that vision's face was grained;
Yet no blood reached there from the upper ground,
And no guns thumped, or down the flues made moan.
"Strange friend," I said, "here is no cause to mourn."
"None," said that other, "save the undone years,
The hopelessness. Whatever hope is yours,
Was my life also; I went hunting wild
After the wildest beauty in the world,
Which lies not calm in eyes, or braided hair,
But mocks the steady running of the hour,
And if it grieves, grieves richlier than here.
For by my glee might many men have laughed,
And of my weeping something had been left,
Which must die now. I mean the truth untold,
The pity of war, the pity war distilled.
Now men will go content with what we spoiled.
Or, discontent, boil bloody, and be spilled.
They will be swift with swiftness of the tigress.
None will break ranks, though nations trek from progress.
Courage was mine, and I had mystery;
Wisdom was mine, and I had mastery:
To miss the march of this retreating world
Into vain citadels that are not walled.
Then, when much blood had clogged their chariot-wheels,
I would go up and wash them from sweet wells,
Even with truths that lie too deep for taint.
I would have poured my spirit without stint
But not through wounds; not on the cess of war.
Foreheads of men have bled where no wounds were.

"I am the enemy you killed, my friend.
I knew you in this dark: for so you frowned
Yesterday through me as you jabbed and killed.
I parried; but my hands were loath and cold.
Let us sleep now. . . ."

This poem has everything for me. T.S. Eliot called it a "technical achievement of great originality" and "one of the most moving pieces of verse inspired by the war." There are lots of critiques regarding Owen's innovative technique, use of pararhyme and use of assonant endings. A strange tale of how a dead soldier descends into hell to meet a slain foe only to realise that in death they are the same, "I am the enemy you killed, my friend."

In my home town of Shrewsbury Owen's name appears on the war memorial in the assembly hall where Owen went to school and where my sons also attended. In the grounds of Shrewsbury Abbey is another memorial. "Symmetry" in commemoration of the life and work of Wilfred Owen. The sculpture is by Paul de Monchaux and was unveiled outside Shrewsbury Abbey in June 1993. The line "I am the enemy you killed" is engraved on one side is from " Strange Meeting". The design echoes the symmetries in Owen's poem as well as the trenches of 1917 and the Sambre-Oise canal in 1918 representing pontoon bridges over the Sambre canal, where Wilfred Owen was killed. The sculpture expresses the significance of the poet as bridge builder and communicator, and the stark shape also represents the structure of the trenches lined with duckboards. Symmetries in the design represent symmetries in Owen's poem strange meeting, from which the inscription is taken. The memorial can also be used as a bench, a safe haven for the weary.

Field with Poppies, Vincent van Gogh

No room for the dead by Bill West

They didn't bring
the dead home
so in 1922 they made
a statue, in the park, an
angel with wings and a flag
suited in armour
St Michael, the archangel.

Penned in by pillars,
balustrade and gate
and covered with a dome, like a
temple, a floor tiled with emblems
of the great and good.

So much neater
than the regiments
of headstones
that would have
filled Shropshire fields.

POETS WHO DIED IN THE WAR

Rupert Brooke - died 23rd April 1915 of blood poisoning following a mosquito bite. Age 28

Julian Grenfell - died of wounds, 30th April 1915. Age 27

Charles Hamilton Sorley - killed 13th October 1915 in the Battle of Loos. Age 20

Robert Palmer - killed 21st January, 1916, in Mesopotamia. Age 28

William Noel Hodgson - killed 1st July 1916 on the first day of the Battle of the Somme. Age 23

Alan Seeger - killed 4th July 1916 in the Battle of the Somme. Age 28

ART: Conversation With God, Linnet Design: Following Nicholas Roerich

Conversation with God, Following Nicholas Roerichm MLF, PS, 2018

Edward Wyndham Tennant - killed 22nd September 1916 in the Battle of the Somme. Age 19

Arthur Graeme West - killed 3rd April 1917 by a sniper. Age 26

Edward Thomas - killed 9th April 1917 in the Battle of Arras. Age 39

Robert Ernest Vernede - killed 9th April, 1917 in an attack on Havrincourt Wood. Age 41

Francis Ledwidge - killed Boezinge, Ypres, 31st July 1917, Age 29

Hedd Wyn - killed on the first day of the Battle of Passchendaele during World War I on 31st July 1917, Age 30

Ewart Alan Mackintosh - killed 21st November, 1917 at Cambrai, Age 24

John McCrae - died of pneumonia, 28th January, 1918. Age 46

Isaac Rosenberg - killed 1st April 1918, on night patro, Age 28

Phillip Bainbrigge - killed 18th September, 1918, Age 27

Wilfred Owen - killed 4th November, 1918, Age 25

In the queue for bread. First World War. Ivan Vladimirov

"It is a serious thing to live in a society of possible gods and goddesses, to remember that the dullest most uninteresting person you can talk to may one day be a creature which,if you saw it now, you would be strongly tempted to worship, or else a horror and a corruption such as you now meet, if at all, only in a nightmare. All day long we are, in some degree helping each other to one or the other of these destinations. It is in the light of these overwhelming possibilities, it is with the awe and the circumspection proper to them, that we should conduct all of our dealings with one another, all friendships, all loves, all play, all politics. There are no ordinary people. You have never talked to a mere mortal. Nations, cultures, arts, civilizations - these are mortal, and their life is to ours as the life of a gnat. But it is immortals whom we joke with, work with, marry, snub, and exploit - immortal horrors or everlasting splendors."

C.S. Lewis, The Weight of Glory

IMAGINING MANY GODS:

SAPPHO, HOMER, AND MARILYN MONROE

Stephen Zelnick

Were the ancients like us? Perhaps people are people and we share their problems and concerns. But suppose what is common for us were alien for them, their experience unfathomable to us? If they were different, our self-understanding could seem limited, maybe nonsensical. Studying the past could be unsettling, perhaps dangerous. Maybe the ancients have something to teach us, things beyond our common understanding. Otherwise, frankly, why bother?

1

Ancient Greeks worshipped many gods. We know the Olympian Deities, both their Greek and Roman names: Zeus (Jupiter); Hera (Juno); Poseidon (Neptune); Hades (Pluto); Aphrodite (Venus); Ares (Mars), Athena (Minerva), Hermes (Mercury), Hephaistos (Vulcan), Apollo (Phoebus Apollo), and Dionysus (Bacchus). The ancients took their gods seriously, both in official ceremonies conducted in central locations by the state, but also in the small village world and at the private hearth. In a pre-technical world, when so many matters were beyond the control of human beings, propitiating the gods seemed sensible, and was as effective then as now.

We believe we are monotheists; and even our atheists vigorously deny the existence of only one god. However, aliens studying us would likely conclude that we worship many gods. Money, power, celebrity, creativity, sexual pleasure, the delight in violence, sociability, and celebration of ourselves – staunch abstinence from all these -- would appear in our Olympian roster ... with "God" lagging behind as a ponderous after-thought. That lonely Abrahamic God is all about restraint (although sometimes Zeus-like, when loosing the fateful lightning), and about the world beyond (when not directing politicians with absolute authority). We may not be so far from polytheism as we think. Suppose we worshipped directly what we worship in our minds and hearts and actions?

Sappho and Homer, both from before the birth of philosophy, can help here. In their time, deities had not yet been subjected to rationality, before human beings had set boundaries on what gods could be, both in their own behavior and in what they could demand from us.

Sappho was born in the seventh century BCE, two centuries before Socrates required the gods to be moral and intellectually consistent and several more centuries before Christianity had consigned most of human nature to the devil. In <u>Republic</u> Socrates condemns the Greek Myths because they portray gods doing immoral and irrational things. Socrates requires gods or God to be rational and decent. Goodness and righteousness, then, are the gods of God – God is all-powerful, but cannot perform un-godly acts. Christianity takes this further, insisting human nature is corrupt and whatever is excellent in us is worthless, without the sanction of Jesus' teaching. 1 Corinthians 13 condemns human powers and accomplishments as "tinkling cymbals and sounding brass" compared with caring for one another and maintaining faith in God. What can we learn from a world before these adjustments and revaluations? If we were devoted to these old Greek gods, what would our lives be like?

[pic]

This is an idealized conception of Sappho. She was born on the Island of Lesbos somewhere around 630 BCE and died around 590. All but a few poems and broken fragments remain from her numerous and popular works. Sappho has become a celebrated figure as an ancient woman artist and lesbian, but the romantic, heroic, and tragic tales of Sappho's life – such as Erica Jong's "Sappho's Leap" (2003) -- are imaginary. This image is an ancient Roman fresco from Pompeii.

3

The library at Alexandria once held nine volumes of Sappho's works. Her poetry was known throughout the Mediterranean; very little survives. Some think the early Christian Church destroyed her works. In any case, we have Sappho's works, once so popular, only as a half dozen reconstructed poems and several dozen fragments, gathered from potshards and mummy wrappings. By happy accident, one Sappho poem was entirely preserved but only because the rhetorician Dionysius of Halicarnassus used it as a textbook example of excellent expression.

In our monotheistic world, Greek gods have become decorative or mere examples of how pre-scientific peoples explained the unexplainable. We delight in those gods and tell their stories to our children to excite their imaginations before they settle down to managing a cost-estimated reality. Still, we retain hints of their powers. Aphrodite (Venus) and her cupids, haunt our dreams, both night and day. Ares (Mars) directs our national policy far more forcefully than Jesus does. Indeed, Ares even guides our business ethic, too, where warfare provides the metaphors for getting ahead. And we invite God to strike us dead – with one of Zeus' (Jupiter's) lightning bolts – when we protest our truthfulness, even while we know God postpones our punishments until the Day of Judgment.

Occasionally, it may occur to us, as it did to Wordsworth ("The World is Too Much with us," 1805) that these gods were real to ancient people. Wordsworth's poem imagines that gods lived in a richly embellished world where our inner experience shared force with all creation, and where the natural world, peopled with Olympian figures, was personified without embarrassment. Before the soul became spiritualized, and bodies demoted to mere means of transportation for spirit, gods spoke to us. In that world all was invested with the energies and intelligences of fabulous beings, and every hill and stream told a story that made them and us magical.

Wordsworth's speaker, in his disgust at having a mind framed by the bland "getting and spending" of his commercial time, bursts out:

> Great God! I'd rather be
> A pagan suckled in a creed outworn;
> So might I, standing on this pleasant lea.
> Have glimpses that would make me less forlorn;
> Have sight of Proteus rising from the sea;
> Or hear old Triton blow his wreathed horn.

The speaker yearns for primitive imagination that sees and hears the ocean gods instead of calculating beach-front rentals as any sensible person would. It is not clear in the poem whether the speaker completes his journey back to the vital perceptions of ancient times. However, the speaker is convinced these gods drove the forces of nature and were once real and palpable to us.

4

The young woman in Sappho's "Hymn to Aphrodite" has that sort of mind. She summons the goddess, who recalls for the poet their intimate relation. Translations vary, but they all emphasize the humorous intimacy between the young woman and the goddess, two girls of like mind conspiring together:

> Undying Aphrodite on your caparisoned throne, Daughter of Zeus and weaver of ruses—
> Now I address you:

41

Queen, do not hurt my heart, do not harry it
But come as before when you heard and you hearkened
A long way away,

And leaving behind the house of your father, harnessed a golden chariot winged
By your beautiful swans,

Beating and whirring across the sky,
Bringing you down to the unbright earth –
So suddenly there:

Mistress, the smile of your undying features
Asking me what was it troubled me this time?
What made me call you

This time? What was my desperate heart wanting done?
And your: "Whom shall I this time bend to your love?
Who is it Sappho

That's doing you wrong? For if she's escaping
Soon she'll be chasing: if she's refusing
Your gifts, she shall give them.

And, if she's not loving, soon shall she love you,
Like it or no."... Oh, come again now:
Let me go loose from this merciless craving.
Do what I long to have done: be my own
Helper in battle.   (trans. Paul Roche)

[pic]

Aphrodite (Venus), detail from Sandro Botticelli's, "The Birth of Venus" (1480s). Though more than half a millennium old, the image is remarkably fresh and modern and not weighted down in stone. It fits nicely the notion in Sappho's poem of a goddess who is familiar, youthful, and jocular. The painting is in the Uffizi Gallery in Florence.

Aphrodite inhabits a brilliant world of "golden" chariots and must be cajoled to abandon her "caparisoned throne" (poikilothrone) to descend to our "unbright earth." Aphrodite is the "Daughter of Zeus", but she is also a "weaver of ruses," (doloploke) a trickster of the heart. Invoked by her devoted Sappho, she is "So suddenly there," and an intimate and humorous conversation ensues.

Aphrodite playfully mocks poor Sappho. The goddess is immortal, her features undying (athanatos); the human lover lives in time, in ragged and demeaning repetition. The goddess has been on this mission before: "what was it troubled me this time? What made me call/This time? .. "Whom shall I this time bend to your love?" The repetition of "this time" (deute) marks a comic exasperation in Aphrodite, the Olympian witness to a human heart captive to vagrant passions. The further question "Who is it Sappho/That's doing you wrong?" contrasts a wise older sister who, with gentle humor, understands distressed desire. Though playful and mocking, the goddess sympathizes with pouting Sappho who counts it a moral wrong if her beloved fails to respond immediately. Though expressed gently here, to be gripped by desire is to abandon judgment and in petulance imagine harm where there is none.

Sappho would have Aphrodite cast a spell on the beloved so that she too will suffer, whether that is good for her, or is in any way deserved. Only these ruses can free Sappho from "this merciless craving." The goddess has no interest in the welfare of the beloved but only in playing those tricks by which desire triumphs. Neither of these conspirators is honest and just; one can transcend this unbright earth, only through the transforming power of desire. Sexual desire is Sappho's religion, Aphrodite is her goddess, and love is the remedy for the dullness of our days and for the sour recognition of our mortality.

5

Aphrodite represents only one of the great forces Greeks celebrated to understand themselves. We can think of these twelve gods as something like the zodiac's distribution of character types. If so, the Greeks seem willing to accept both joys and pains that come with intense devotion to any one of these mighty beings. Our horoscopes, in contrast, allow for mixed types and rarely require us to pay the bitter price for the unalloyed gifts of nature. As Nietzsche protested, moralism exalted restraint to elevate moral consistency (serving the community, sometimes expressed as the state). This means that all human potentials other than moral consistency and administered goodness are secondary to moderation. Nietzsche mocked this narrowing of the palette of values. If Aphrodite is to be eclipsed by the need for administrative order, the world turns gray and dismal. Banish Sappho, banish all the world.
[pic]

Athena (Minerva) is the goddess of war and wisdom, which seems at first peculiar. However, there is much wisdom associated with war if we think of strategy as a necessary element. Athena was also goddess of weaving, a domestic art closely associated with strategy if we think of the foresight required to produce the image in a tapestry as it takes form on a loom.

43

That the Church set out to outlaw Sappho's poetry should not surprise us. The Greek gods represent variety in human nature, each kind of soul supported by a god or goddess to whom devotees could give their all. Some of us are Ares (Mars) people, some belong to Hephaistos (Vulcan), and some, like Sappho, are children of Aphrodite (Venus). Think of Odysseus and his relation to Athena (Minerva). Athena is devoted to Odysseus because he dedicates himself to her without reserve. He has an "Athenan" soul. He is quick-witted, a master strategist, an aggressive man who keeps calm, even in the face of terrifying monsters. What Athena weaves in fabric, Odysseus weaves in action. Who of us could invent, while gazing into the horrifying face of Polyphemus (the Cyclops), the remarkable trick of calling himself "No Man"? Such craftiness is beyond human powers, except for a human assisted by his personal goddess. This undivided devotion makes Odysseus what he is, both his stunning prowess and his troubled restlessness. He possesses a hero's character; he serves neither the welfare of his crew, the safety of his family, or the needs of Ithaca. His brilliance is to be, full-force, the man he is.

Let us recall the story of Odysseus and the Cyclops from The Odyssey (Book IX). Coming upon an unfamiliar group of islands, Odysseus decides to leave behind eleven of his ships. He then selects twelve of his best warriors to go exploring. They come upon an empty cave, clearly inhabited by a shepherd who produces cheese in great abundance and help themselves. When this shepherd returns, Odysseus and his crew are horrified to discover that he is the one-eyed giant Polyphemus ("much spoken of"). The Cyclops drives his flock inside, and then blocks the entrance with an immense stone, trapping the intruders inside. Polyphemus soon discovers his unwelcomed guests, seizes two of them by the legs, dashes out their brains, and devours them. The brave crew is terrified and can see no way to escape their cannibal captor. Command of their courage and their wits is not improved when, upon awakening, the Cyclops breakfasts upon two more crewmen before shepherding out his flock to graze and resealing the mouth of the cave.

Although others have abandoned their wits to terror, Odysseus remains cool and devises a plan. His solution demonstrates just why he is the favorite of Athena, goddess of strategic warfare and weaving. This pairing of skills might first strike us as strange, one so masculine and the other associated with domestic tasks, but they are intimately related. For the pattern to appear in any complex tapestry, the weaver must be able to foresee, hundreds of threadings ahead, where the emerging pattern will go. Similarly, a plan of battle is a weaving of men and materials into reality. Odysseus is Athena's favorite precisely because he is so skilled at strategy; and because he is so skilled, Athena guides his fate in the world. His superb potential is realized fully with the assistance of his goddess. Put another way, the cunning demonstrated by Odysseus in defeating Polyphemus exceeds the capability of all but a very few. He is that one among us -- think of your childhood gang of friends -- who says, "I know what we can do," and is correct while the rest of us stand by in confusion. How can we account for this precocity? Surely, our capable friend is favored by Athena and is learning to perfect this aptitude, which is the gift of the goddess. How else account for such prowess, executed by a mere mortal like ourselves?

Looking about the cave, Odysseus notices a sizable log, still green with sap, and orders his quaking crewmen to sharpen one end to a keen point, and then harden the point over a blazing fire. But his crewmen could well ask: "what good is that?" Polyphemus is a giant of immense strength, and no bulky weapon of this sort can be wielded effectively by puny mortals. His crew cannot be encouraged when after the Cyclops returns at the end of his day, he finishes off his meal by devouring two more of Odysseus' men for dessert. Well fed, and happy with his pantry of human delicacies, Polyphemus enjoys Odysseus' obsequious gesture in offering him a fine wine brought from afar. The crude shepherd delights in this delicacy and graciously rewards his guest, Odysseus, with a special gift. When Polyphemus asks

Odysseus his name, Odysseus tells him his name is "no man" ("me tis"). Having drunk his fill, Polyphemus reveals his malice; the gift will be that "me tis" will be eaten last, and the monster roars with laughter at his grim trickery. Things appear hopeless, especially if we have forgotten that sharpened stake, but Odysseus has not.

When the giant, having enjoyed Odysseus' gift, collapses into drunken slumber, Odysseus orders his men into action. Shouldering the huge log, they plunge its smoldering point into the single eye of the Cyclops. In agony, the blinded giant rushes from his cave bellowing for assistance from his Cyclopean neighbors. But all he can tell them is that "no man" (me tis) has injured him, and so his neighbors depart. Next morning, Odysseus and his men leave by grasping the undersides of blind Polyphemus' rams, so he cannot detect them as they escape. The least alert reader will marvel at the wit of "no man" whose adopted name in Greek ("metis") also means "cunning" ("Metis" the name of Athena's mother – Homer is also a cunning weaver). How can we fail to marvel at the Olympian powers of someone who grasps his identity so firmly?

[pic]

No one knows what Homer looked like, and some doubt he even was a particular person and not the name associated with a tradition of tales. Tradition has it that he was blind, based upon a self-referential passage citing a blind personage. If the figure of Hephaistos in the "Iliad" is the clue I believe it is, "Homer" has left a strong thumb-print on his great portrait of war and its passions.

7

Elsewhere we find, in Homer himself, a very different kind of soul and devotion. In Book One of The Iliad Homer depicts a festive gathering of the Olympian gods. While they dine on the nectar only gods can taste, we notice that these immortals are waited upon by a limping figure, Hephaistos, who though a god himself, is diminished by his injuries. The story of his humiliating injury, at the hands of Zeus evokes our pity. Hephaistos found himself caught between his mother Hera and Zeus' rage towards his saucy wife. In attempting to protect her, Hephaistos is hurled from heaven in a fall so profound it takes three days. He is crippled ever after and doomed to serve the luminous beings that populate Olympus.

Homer's Hephaistos is noble; the mockery directed at him by his glorious superiors hateful and mean:

> [Hephaistos] spoke, and the goddess of the white arms Hera smiled at him,
> And smiling she accepted the goblet out of her son's hand.

Thereafter beginning from the left he poured drinks for the other
Gods, dipping up from the mixing bowl the sweet nectar.
But among the blessed immortals uncontrollable laughter
went up as they saw Hephaistos bustling about the palace. (Bk I, 595-600)

(Trans Fitzgerald)

His service to them, as well as his broken gait, makes him an object of ridicule. Homer underscores how unjust this is when he tells us that these cruel aristocrats in their exquisite leisure retire to palaces Hephaistos built for them:

Afterwards, when the light of the flaming sun went under
they went away each one to sleep in his home where
for each one the far-renowned strong-handed Hephaistos
had built a house by means of his craftsmanship and cunning. (Bk I, 605-608)

[pic]

In this image from a Greek vase, the river goddess Thetis appeals to Hephaistos to create the magical shield for her son, Achilles. The shield as described in Book XVIII of the "Iliad", a work of bronze and gold, reflects the art of the poet in bringing human figures to life through words alone.

We may wonder how Hephaistos could serve as a divinity that excites one's soul to emulation and provides strength to guide one's life and actions. He is unpleasant in appearance and has been reduced to humble servitude. And yet, Hephaistos is a divinity, and has won the devotion of Homer himself. Hephaistos, the god of craftsmanship, is Homer's god. We think of poets benefitting from their muses, those wispy beings that inspire them. However, Homer knows that poets execute a craft as demanding as silversmiths and sculptors and metal-workers at their forge. Like Hephaistos, Homer possesses the extraordinary powers to lend the appearance of life to mere objects with his magical craft.

Homer introduces Hephaistos at the end of Book One of The Iliad, a position of special emphasis. Hephaistos does not re-appear until the critical moment (Book 18) when Achilleus, enraged by the death of his beloved comrade Patroklus, forsakes his brooding and decides to re-enter the war. Patroklus had been wearing the battle-armor of Achilleus, and Hektor, a Trojan hero of prodigious strength, has carried the armor away as a prize of war. Achilleus tells his mother, the river goddess Thetis, that he accepts his doom, the fate that he will succeed in killing Hektor but will die soon after. Thetis, who cared for the injured Hephaistos when he was tossed from the heavens out of Olympus, travels to Hephaistos' dark underworld workshop to enlist his help in fashioning new armor for her son. Homer then devotes 130 lines (Bk. XVIII, 478-608) to describing the embellishments of the famous shield of Achilleus.

While many have commented on this brilliant passage, Homer wants us to link the skill of Hephaistos with his own. Multiple sets of people appear on the shield, each engaged in a separate drama. In one panel, two cities are depicted. One celebrates a marriage festival:

> They were leading the brides along the city from their maiden chambers
> under the flaring of torches, and the loud bride song was arising.
> The young men followed the circles of the dance and among them
> the flutes and lyres kept up their clamour as in the meantime
> the women standing each at the door of her court admired them.

The figures are seen, but somehow also heard, and they are also in motion, and they interact with one another. What skill is required to bring these inanimate figures alive!

The second panel depicts a complex war narrative, including an elaborate account of strategies: one scene gives way to another in a complex thread of implication and result. Given that this narrative must be contained within a limited space, we are hard pressed to know how this could be done. The details of the battle alone show the shifts of fortune as victory tilts from one side to the other. In the end Homer tells us: "All closed together like living men and fought with each other/ and dragged away from each other the corpses of those who had fallen" (540-541). Although depicted in brass and gold, they are "like living men" and extend their efforts to arduous battle. Unlike Keats' "Ode on a Grecian Urn" where the figures are static and their motion and imagined sound happen only in the mind of the viewer, the figures on the shield of Achilleus are blessed with sound and motion and acquire the space for a complex narrative.

Who but a god could command such magic? Homer accomplishes that in The Iliad, where a reality unfolds before us in mere words. Through Homer's craftsmanship we experience all the drama of the "ringing plains of windy Troy": the sound and mayhem of battle, the inner worlds of those who die, the glory in the taste of victory, and the acid of humiliation for those who fail the test of courage. Hephaistos is lame and disfigured but creates gods and heroes out of metal and fire. Homer, a blind poet, makes his heroes live again and makes us see them.

8

Sappho creates brilliant poetry by embracing the goddess Aphrodite, without restraint. Odysseus triumphs over monstrous giants and the menacing vengeance of Poseidon by shaping himself to the powers of Athena. Homer's devotion to Hephaistos, the humiliated god of craftsmanship, allows him to make his narrative, his characters, and the drama of his scenes come alive. None of these devotions are anything like those advanced by Christianity. For the Christian world, these devotions are Faustian pacts with devils by which human beings trade their immortal souls to acquire super-human powers.

[pic]

If you doubt that human beings, aided by the gods, walk among us, consider the luminous qualities of such as Michael Jordan, Pablo Picasso, Steve Jobs, and the incomparable Marilyn Monroe. Some of us are more than mere mortals.

It must be that the Greeks noticed among them individuals who possessed extraordinary skills and powers. How account, in our world, for a Michael Jordan who possesses the power of flight, levitating gracefully beyond gravity? Isn't it clear that Hermes blessed him? To what god did Picasso pay his devotions so that every stroke of his brush would fascinate us? Didn't we see Hephaistos hovering above Steve Jobs? What price did Aphrodite exact so that Norma Jean would rise from the waves as Marilyn Monroe? What would your life be were you able to identify which god resides in you and commit to that god with absolute devotion?

9

The suspicion that Christianity erased Sappho from cultural memory is plausible. Her fierce dedication to Aphrodite swept aside all else, including fairness to the object of her desire and her own stability. The cunning powers of Odysseus to trick others by his words, earned him a place deep in Dante's Inferno, not far from Satan himself, the father of lies. The energy of his restless seeking, and the construction of his heroic self, count for nothing in the Christian world where humility and service to God and others is paramount. The artist devoted solely to his creations becomes a mad scientist in the Christian world, as in Hawthorne's "Rappaccini's Daughter." Aphrodite rewards Pygmalion for investing stone with the force of his longing; in our world, Dr. Frankenstein is punished for reaching beyond the world God made.

The core Christian statement of this hostility to the gods of the ancient world and their powers appears in 1 Corinthians 13. This magnificent rhapsody by the Apostle Paul celebrates caring (charity; love) above all else. The power of rhetoric, so prized among the ancients, is worth little; speaking "with the tongues of mortals and angels" has no value if caring is absent. "Prophetic powers" and understanding of "all mysteries and all knowledge" is worthless without the humble acceptance that all human knowledge is imperfect and will be eclipsed by revelation. Aggression, self-confidence, and heroic self-assertion are insignificant compared with "faith, hope, and charity." Christianity celebrates the comfort and stability of the community under God's law of perfect love, and rejects the assertions of heroic self-seeking, whether the field is war, the arts, the pursuit of knowledge, or pleasure.

10

Were the Greeks religious? They slaughtered prized animals to offer them to these gods (once they stopped sacrificing their children); they made perilous journeys to distant sacred sites; in frenzies, they mutilated their bodies; they built elaborate shrines at great costs, supported a powerful and expensive priesthood; made life choices based upon auguries; and solidified communal values in deeply felt rituals. Is this religion or fairy stories?

Sappho's devotional poetry, then, poses serious challenges for us, her late and alien admirers. What does it mean to devote oneself without restraint to Aphrodite? While we hope our political and military leaders are steeped in goodness, we expect them also to be cunning strategists, able to face down the monsters that threaten us. In the creations of our most gifted artists we are offered glimpses of perfection. What does it cost us to respond without limit and the normal orderly protections of moderated desire? How do we imagine respect for a fellow human being who is a daughter, or son, of Aphrodite, Athena, or Hephaistos? In the face of these differences, we are forced to consider what has become of our gods and goddesses. And who are we without them? In the absence of such gods, what things or thoughts or powers can make our unbright earth shine? And how would we worship them?

—

This quiet Dust was Gentlemen and Ladies
by Emily Dickinson

This quiet Dust was Gentlemen and Ladies
And lads and girls;
Was laughter and ability and sighing,
And frocks and curls;

This passive place a summer's nimble mansion,
Where bloom and bees
Fulfilled their oriental circuit,
Then ceased like these.

"STANDING BY"

The " Blues."

ENCYCLOPAEDIA OF MILITARY TERMS
ATTENTION (pronounced " Stun ").

This is one of the most wonderful words in the military language. It is never spoken or whispered, it is always shouted, bellowed, shrieked, or screamed. Just according to the lung power of the officer or N.C.O. in charge of the squad or party which is to be drilled, paraded, fed, "clinked," washed, or (occasionally) paid. The effects of the command " Shun " on a battalion is both electrical and hypnotic. It is probably the only magic word now in use that was used in the days of Aladdin and his lamp. Should a poker game be in progress and the fabulous stakes be piled chin high on the dug-out or hut floor, until the scene resembles Monte Carlo or Dawson City, and an officer appears, some one utters the magic word "Shun," and the dug-out is immediately transformed into a Sister Susie sewing class, not a nickel or an ace can be seen. The officer usually says "Carry on," and out come chess boards, Psalm books, knitting needles, woodbines, mouth organs, writing material, girls' photographs, The Listening Post, and gingerbeer. "What did you say, Editor? Get on with the 'cyclopaedia. Very good, Sir." Sir Robert Ball and the Vancouver Sun say that if Halley's Comet comes within one million miles of this earth, everything will be as quiet as the "German Navy." We're taking some awful chances when we say it, but the word " Shun " when a General or Colonel is on parade has got Halley's Comet beat fifty different ways as a silencer. From The Listening Post.

(Continued)
DUG-OUT. A hole in the ground with a lid on.
There are three kinds of dug-outs at the front. The
"Bungalow" for Officers, the " Love in a Cottage"
for Sergeants, and the " Noah's Ark " for privates.
They are built for men, mice, rats, and cats to
sleep in. A dug-out is decorated with jam, cheese,
photographs, and fleas.

DAM. This is what the Engineers do to a river or
  "Ford." By simply adding the letter " N " we
have a suitable prefix for use when referring to the
Kaiser, the weather, a heavy pack, a route march, a
  dirty rifle, a working party, a leaky dug-out, and
barbed wire, etc. It is used unhesitatingly by all
troops excepting the Padre, his nearest approach
  being " Darned."

DRESSING STATION. The home of pills,
  poultices, plasters, cascarettes, castor oil, and
catgut, needles, knives, and "nerves."

DEFAULTER. A man who has made up his
  mind to be more careful "next time."

"And the WOODBINE spices are wafted abroad."
TENNYSON.

(Continued)

BARBED WIRE: Some one has written that this was invented by Mephisto. After what we have heard about him it is surprising that he should invent anything of such an affectionate and " clinging" nature. At the front it is used for giving an artistic finish to a trench. No trench is complete without it. It is planted at night in order that the artillery may plough it up in the morning. A good crop of barbed wire has been known to prevent opposing armies from arguing the " point." When a soldier gets tangled up in it he says things which are not taught at school. This may be the reason why the Padre never goes on a wiring party or leads an attack.

BILLET: On active service a billet may be anything from a shed to a chateau. Usually the former. When troops are to be moved from one part of the front to another, a billeting party is sent in advance. These men receive explicit instructions to locate the most draughty and leaky barns in the country. At this they are experts. The generous-hearted farmers then inform their cattle and pigs that they must be very polite and wipe their feet before walking over a brave soldier's blankets. He also gives the hens and chickens warning not to lay eggs where a soldier may crush them. The farmer's wife then pours a jug of beer into a barrel of water, his daughters practise a " No compres" smile and everything is ready for the reception of the "Soldat Canadien." From The Listening Post.

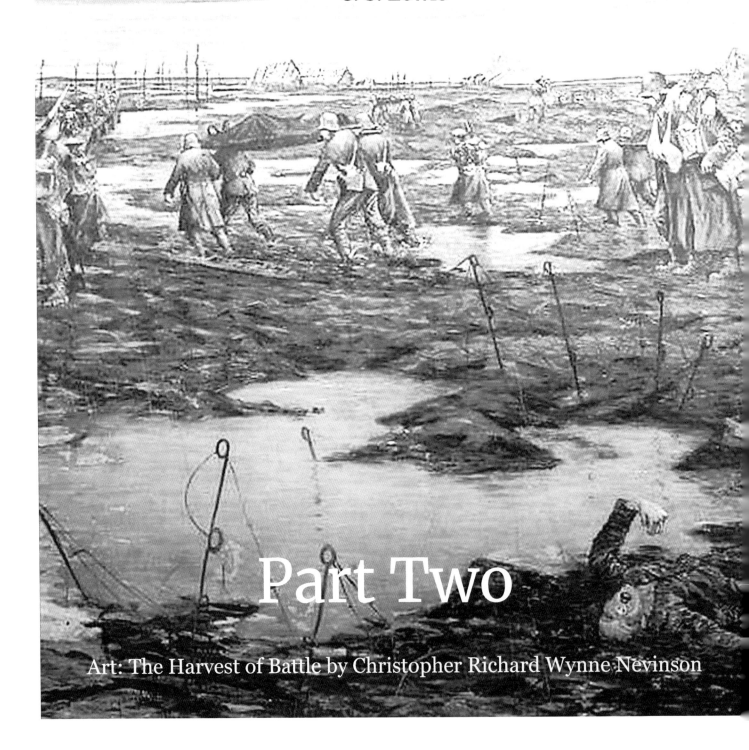

This is one of the miracles of love: It gives a
power of seeing through its own
enchantments and yet not being
disenchanted.
C. S. Lewis

Part Two

Art: The Harvest of Battle by Christopher Richard Wynne Nevinson

Smile, Smile, Smile
By Wilfred Owen

Head to limp head, the sunk-eyed wounded scanned
Yesterday's *Mail*; the casualties (typed small)
And (large) Vast Booty from our Latest Haul.
Also, they read of Cheap Homes, not yet planned;
"For," said the paper, "when this war is done
The men's first instinct will be making homes.
Meanwhile their foremost need is aerodromes,
It being certain war has just begun.
Peace would do wrong to our undying dead,—
The sons we offered might regret they died
If we got nothing lasting in their stead.
We must be solidly indemnified.
Though all be worthy Victory which all bought.
We rulers sitting in this ancient spot
Would wrong our very selves if we forgot
The greatest glory will be theirs who fought,
Who kept this nation in integrity."
Nation?—The half-limbed readers did not chafe
But smiled at one another curiously
Like secret men who know their secret safe.
(This is the thing they know and never speak,
That England one by one had fled to France
Not many elsewhere now save under France).
Pictures of these broad smiles appear each week,
And people in whose voice real feeling rings
Say: How they smile! They're happy now, poor things.

Peace
By Rupert Brooke

Now, God be thanked who has matched us with his hour,
    And caught our youth, and wakened us from sleeping!
With hand made sure, clear eye, and sharpened power,
    To turn, as swimmers into cleanness leaping,
Glad from a world grown old and cold and weary;
    Leave the sick hearts that honor could not move,
And half-men, and their dirty songs and dreary,
    And all the little emptiness of love!
Oh! we, who have known shame, we have found release there,
    Where there's no ill, no grief, but sleep has mending,
        Naught broken save this body, lost but breath;
Nothing to shake the laughing heart's long peace there,
    But only agony, and that has ending;
        And the worst friend and enemy is but Death.

Prayer for Those on the Staff
Julian Grenfell, 1888–1915

Fighting in mud, we turn to Thee,
In these dread times of battle, Lord.
To keep us safe, if so may be,
From shrapnel, snipers, shell, and sword.

But not on us, for we are men
Of meaner clay, who fight in clay,
but on the Staff, the Upper Ten,
Depends the issue of the Day.

The staff is working with its brains,
While we are sitting in the trench;
The Staff the universe ordains
(subject to Thee and General French).

God help the staff-especially
The young ones, many of them sprung
From our high aristocracy;
Their task is hard, and they are young.

O Lord, who mad'st all things to be,
And madest some things very good,
Please keep the Extra A.D.C.
From horrid scenes, and sight of blood.

See that his eggs are newly laid,
Not tinged as some of them-with green;
And let no nasty draughts invade
The windows of his Limousine.

When he forgets to buy the bread,
When there are no more minerals,
Preserve his smooth well-oiled head
From wrath of caustic Generals.

O Lord, who mad'st all things to be,
And hatest nothing thou has made,
Please keep the Extra A.D.C
Out of the sun and in the shade.

To Germany
Charles Hamilton Sorley, 1895–1915

You are blind like us. Your hurt no man designed,
And no man claimed the conquest of your land.
But gropers both through fields of thought confined
We stumble and we do not understand.
You only saw your future bigly planned,
And we, the tapering paths of our own mind,
And in each other's dearest ways we stand,
And hiss and hate. And the blind fight the blind.

When it is peace, then we may view again
With new-won eyes each other's truer form
And wonder. Grown more loving-kind and warm
We'll grasp firm hands and laugh at the old pain,
When it is peace. But until peace, the storm
The darkness and the thunder and the rain.

"Ir is only when men are drawn out of self
by love of those near and dear to them that
their souls are turned to catch the finer
appeal to a wider and more arduous self-
sacrifice, and so become able to rise succes-
sively by stepping-stones of their dead selves
to higher things."

R. S. A. PALMER, 1888-1916

Before Action
William Noel Hodgson

By all the glories of the day
And the cool evening's benison
By that last sunset touch that lay
Upon the hills when day was done,
By beauty lavishly outpoured
And blessings carelessly received,
By all the days that I have lived
Make me a soldier, Lord.

By all of all man's hopes and fears
And all the wonders poets sing,
The laughter of unclouded years,
And every sad and lovely thing;
By the romantic ages stored
With high endeavour that was his,
By all his mad catastrophes
Make me a man, O Lord.

I, that on my familiar hill
Saw with uncomprehending eyes
A hundred of thy sunsets spill
Their fresh and sanguine sacrifice,
Ere the sun swings his noonday sword
Must say good-bye to all of this; -
By all delights that I shall miss,
Help me to die, O Lord.

I Have a Rendezvous with Death

Alan Seeger, 1888–1916

I have a rendezvous with Death
At some disputed barricade,
When Spring comes back with rustling shade
And apple-blossoms fill the air—
I have a rendezvous with Death
When Spring brings back blue days and fair.

It may be he shall take my hand
And lead me into his dark land
And close my eyes and quench my breath—
It may be I shall pass him still.
I have a rendezvous with Death
On some scarred slope of battered hill,
When Spring comes round again this year
And the first meadow-flowers appear.

God knows 'twere better to be deep
Pillowed in silk and scented down,
Where Love throbs out in blissful sleep,
Pulse nigh to pulse, and breath to breath,
Where hushed awakenings are dear ...
But I've a rendezvous with Death
At midnight in some flaming town,
When Spring trips north again this year,
And I to my pledged word am true,
I shall not fail that rendezvous.

Re-Incarnation

Edward Wyndham Tennant

I too remember distant golden days
When even my soul was young; I see the sand
Whirl in a blinding pillar towards the band
Of orange sky-line 'neath a turquoise blaze.
Some burnt-out sky spread o'er a glistening land
And slim brown jargoning men in blue and gold
I know it all so well, I understand
The ecstasy of worship ages-old.

Hear the first truth; The great far-seeing soul
Is ever in the humblest husk; I see
How each succeeding section takes its toll
In fading cycles of old memory,
And each new life the life shall control
Until perfection reach Eternity.

The End of the Second Year

Arthur Graeme West

One writes to ask me if I've read
Of "the Jutland battle," of "the great advance
Made by the Russians," chiding—"History
Is being made these days, these are the things
That are worth while."
                                        These!
                                                    Not to one who's lain
In Heaven before God's throne with eyes abased,
Worshipping Him, in many forms of Good,
That sate thereon; turning this patchwork world
Wholly to glorify Him, point His plan
Toward some supreme perfection, dimly visioned
By loving faith: not these to him, when, stressed
By some soul-dizzying woe beyond his trust,
He lifts his startled face, and finds the Throne
Empty, turns away, too drunk with Truth
To mind his shame, or feel the loss of God.

Setting out (1913)

Ernst Stadler

There was a time before, when fanfares bloodily tore
apart my own impatient brain,
So that, up-rearing like a horse, it bit savagely
at the rein.
Then tambourines sounded the alarm on every
path
And a hail of bullets seemed like the loveliest music on earth.
Then, suddenly, life stood still. Different paths were
leading between the old trees.
Rooms were tempting. It was sweet to linger and sweet to
rest at ease,
And, unchaining my body from reality, like some old
dusty armour,
To nestle voluptuously in the down of soft dream-
hour.
But then one morning through the misty air there rolled
the echo of the bugle's ring.
Hard, sharp, whistling like a sword-thrust. As if suddenly
on darkness lights had started shining.
As if, through the tented dawn, trumpet-jolts had roused
the sleeping forces,
The waking soldiers leapt up and struck their tents and
busily harnessed their horses.
I was locked into lines like splints that thrust into
morning, with fire on helmet and stirrup,
Forward, with battle in my blood and in my eyes, and
reins held up.
Perhaps in the evening, victory marches would play
around my head.
Perhaps we all would lie somewhere, stretched out among
the dead.
But before the reaching out and before the sinking,
Our eyes would see their fill of world and sun, and take it
in, glowing and drinking.

65

Leaving For The Front
Alfred Lichtenstein

Before I die, I must just find this rhyme.
Be quiet, my friends, and do not waste any time.

We're marching off in company with death.
I only wish my girl would hold her breath.

There's nothing wrong with me, I'm glad to leave,
Now mother's crying too, there's no reprieve.

And now look how the sun's begun to set.
A nice mass-grave is all that I shall get.

Once more the good old sunset's glowing red.
In thirteen days I'll probably be dead.

(1889-1914)

To Our Fallen

Robert Ernest Vernede

YE sleepers, who will sing you?
We can but give our tears—
Ye dead men, who shall bring you
Fame in the coming years?
Brave souls ... but who remembers
The flame that fired your embers? ...
Deep, deep the sleep that holds you
Who one time had no peers.

Yet maybe Fame's but seeming
And praise you'd set aside,
Content to go on dreaming,
Yea, happy to have died
If of all things you prayed for—
All things your valour paid for—
One prayer is not forgotten,
One purchase not denied.

But God grants your dear England
A strength that shall not cease
Till she have won for all the Earth
From ruthless men release,
And made supreme upon her
Mercy and Truth and Honour—
Is this the thing you died for?
Oh, Brothers, sleep in peace!

(1875-1917)

The Dead Kings
Francis Ledwidge, 1887–1917

All the dead kings came to me
At Rosnaree, where I was dreaming,
A few stars glimmered through the morn,
And down the thorn the dews were streaming.

And every dead king had a story
Of ancient glory, sweetly told.
It was too early for the lark,
But the starry dark had tints of gold.

I listened to the sorrows three
Of that Eire passed into song.
A cock crowed near a hazel croft,
And up aloft dim larks winged strong.

And I, too, told the kings a story
Of later glory, her fourth sorrow:
There was a sound like moving shields
In high green fields and the lowland furrow.

And one said: 'We who yet are kings
Have heard these things lamenting inly.'
Sweet music flowed from many a bill
And on the hill the morn stood queenly.

And one said: 'Over is the singing,
And bell bough ringing, whence we come;
With heavy hearts we'll tread the shadows,
In honey meadows birds are dumb.'

And one said: 'Since the poets perished
And all they cherished in the way,
Their thoughts unsung, like petal showers
Inflame the hours of blue and grey.'

And one said: 'A loud tramp of men
We'll hear again at Rosnaree.'
A bomb burst near me where I lay.
I woke, 'twas day in Picardy.

War
Hed Wyn

Woe that I live in bitter days,
As God is setting like a sun
And in his place, as lord and slave,
Man raises forth his heinous throne.

When he thought God was gone at last
He put his brother to the sword.
Now death is roaring in our ears,
Shadowing the shanties of the poor.

The old and silenced harps are hung
On yonder willow trees again.
The bawl of boys is on the wind.
Their blood is blended in the rain.

Ellis Evans, 1887-1917

Rhyfel
Hed Wyn

Gwae fi fy myw mewn oes mor ddreng
A Duw ar drai ar orwel pell;
O'i ôl mae dyn, yn deyrn a gwreng,
Yn codi ei awdurdod hell.

Pan deimlodd fyned ymaith Dduw
Cyfododd gledd i ladd ei frawd;
Mae swn yr ymladd ar ein clyw,
A'i gysgod ar fythynnod tlawd.

Mae'r hen delynau genid gynt
Ynghrog ar gangau'r helyg draw,
A gwaedd y bechgyn lond y gwynt,
A'u gwaed yn gymysg efo'r glaw.

Ellis Evans, 1887-1917

The Volunteer
E. Alan Mackintosh

I took my heart from the fire of love,
   Molten and warm not yet shaped clear,
And tempered it to steel of proof
   Upon the anvil block of fear.

With steady hammer-strokes I made
   A weapon ready for the fight,
And fashioned like a dagger-blade
   Narrow and pitiless and bright.

Cleanly and tearlessly it slew,
   But as the heavy days went on
The fire that once had warmed it grew
   Duller, and presently was gone.

Oh, innocence and lost desire,
   I strive to kindle it in vain,
Dead embers of a greying fire.
   I cannot melt my heart again.

(1893 - 1917)

In Flanders Fields

John McCrae

In Flanders fields the poppies blow
Between the crosses, row on row,
   That mark our place; and in the sky
   The larks, still bravely singing, fly
Scarce heard amid the guns below.

We are the Dead. Short days ago
We lived, felt dawn, saw sunset glow,
   Loved and were loved, and now we lie,
     In Flanders fields.

Take up our quarrel with the foe:
To you from failing hands we throw
   The torch; be yours to hold it high.
   If ye break faith with us who die
We shall not sleep, though poppies grow
     In Flanders fields.

1872–1918

Returning, We Hear Larks

Isaac Rosenberg

Sombre the night is.
And though we have our lives, we know
What sinister threat lurks there.

Dragging these anguished limbs, we only know
This poison-blasted track opens on our camp –
On a little safe sleep.

But hark! joy – joy – strange joy.
Lo! heights of night ringing with unseen larks.
Music showering our upturned list'ning faces.

Death could drop from the dark
As easily as song –
But song only dropped,
Like a blind man's dreams on the sand
By dangerous tides,
Like a girl's dark hair for she dreams no ruin lies there,
Or her kisses where a serpent hides.

(1890-1918)

If I Should Die

Philip Bainbrigge

If I should die, be not concerned to know
   The manner of my ending, if I fell
Leading a folorn charge against the foe,
   Strangled by gas, or shattered by a shell.
Nor seek to see me in this death-in-life
   Mid shirks and curse, oaths and blood and sweat,
Cold in the darkness, on the edge of strife,
   Bored and afraid, irresolute, and wet

But if you think of me, remember one
   Who loved good dinners, curious parody,
Swimming, and lying naked in the sun,
   Latin hexameters, and heraldry,
Athenian subtleties of dhz and poiz,
   Beethoven, Botticelli, beer, and boys.

(1891-1918)

Sounds of Ellul
Robert Ziegel

A black and rainy evening
With vague feelings of fear
Alive with garish shrieking
Of shots both far and near.
What bring you, laughing soldier
To my heart's dark command
When I, pensive and sober,
In my own grave do stand

What strange column unmoving
Appears with such dark dread?
— Oh, friends you are still living! —
Death, is your realm not fed?

At home with pious greeting
Loved ones the graves do search
Where are the dead now meeting?
The wind blows o'er the church

Death touches grave and heather
And sings: "This have I done."
Perhaps from my eyes forever
Night will now hide the sun.

1895-1916

Prayer Before Battle

Alfred Lichtenstein

The soldiers pray fervently, every man for himself:
God, protect me from bad luck.
Father, son and holy ghost,
Please don't let any shells hit me,
Or those scoundrels, our enemies
Imprison or shoot me,
Don't let me kick the bucket like a dog
For the dear Fatherland.

See, I would like to still live
Milk cows, bang girls,
And beat up that rascal, Sepp.
And get boozed up many times
Before I meet my holy end.
See, I'll pray well and willingly
Say seven rosaries daily,
If, God, in your mercy
You kill my friends Huber or Meier
But spare me.
But if I've got to take it
Let me not be wounded too heavily.
Send me a light leg-wound,
A small arm injury,
So that I return home as a hero
Who can tell many a story.

(1889-1914)

The Cherry Trees by Edward Thomas
(1878-1917)

The cherry trees bend over and are shedding
On the old road where all that passed are dead,
Their petals, strewing the grass as for a wedding
This early May morn when there is none to wed.

Spring in the Trenches by Paul Nash

IWM

"The truth is, of course, that what one regards as interruptions are precisely one's life."

CS Lewis

Part Three

Paths of Glory by Christopher Richard Wynne Nevinson

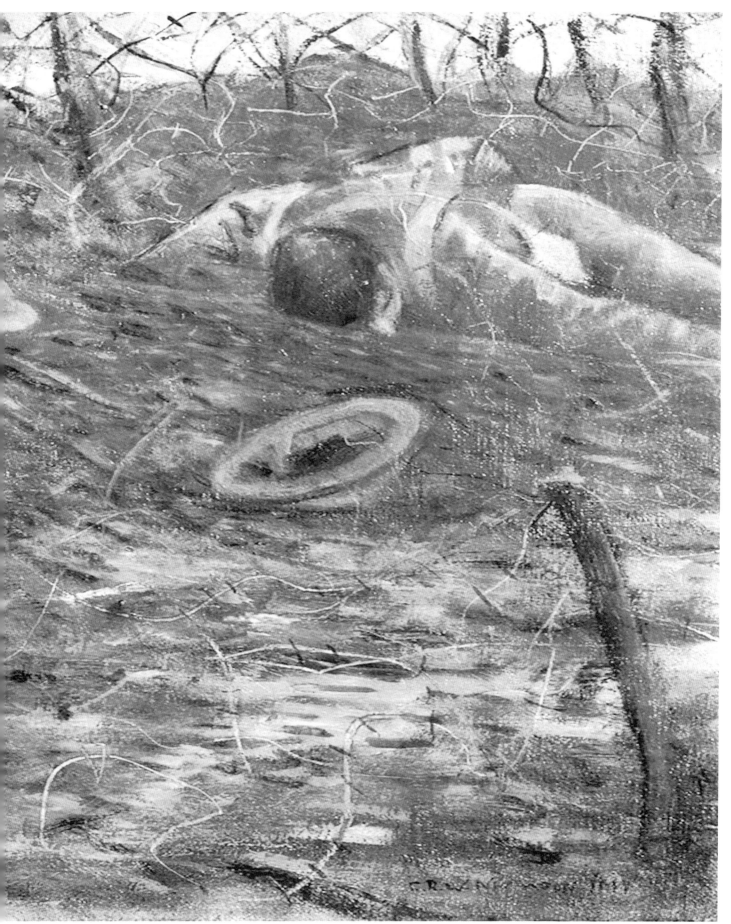

A Song without Words by John William Godward, Date: 1919

On "Everyone Sang": Editorial by Oonah V Joslin

Everyone Sang
by Siegfried Sassoon

Everyone suddenly burst out singing;
And I was filled with such delight
As prisoned birds must find in freedom,
Winging wildly across the white
Orchards and dark-green fields; on - on - and out of sight.

Everyone's voice was suddenly lifted;
And beauty came like the setting sun:
My heart was shaken with tears; and horror
Drifted away ... O, but Everyone
Was a bird; and the song was wordless; the singing will never be done.

Has it ever happened to you? A spontaneous combustion of song? It has to me and I have never forgotten the wonder of that experience. We were a family of singers, and maybe that's part of why I love this poem. But as I became more familiar with it, I was struck more and more by an essence it embodies. I'll call it 'birdness'.

At the beginning of the 20th Century, it was an accustomed thing that communal singing took place. The men in the trenches would have sung around a piano at home or in the pub, sung marching songs in training, and popular songs like Pack Up Your Troubles and of course hymns in church. Church attendance was high. Belief in God and Country walked hand in hand. It was only natural then, they should sing to lift their spirits and Siegfried Sassoon would have been familiar with this so:

Everyone suddenly burst out singing;
And I was filled with such delight

probably really happened at some point. On the face of it, this is a simple statement of joy, and the poem reads almost as an armistice celebration taking place on the battlefield, but it is not that. "Everyone Sang" is dated 12/4/19.

On 13 July 1918, Sassoon was wounded by friendly fire near Arras. As a result, he spent the remainder of the war in England. The poem plays to an audience of people celebrating the end of the war and a return to normal life but there is something much rarer, more poignant, more telling in this poem.

Before the war he led a fairly privileged life. He left Cambridge without a degree. He had a small private income. He liked to write poetry. In A Mystic as Soldier he says:

I lived my days apart,
Dreaming fair songs for God;

not of God but for God, mind you. He believed in God and Country and took his beliefs as seriously as any other. The war changed all that. It made him question what happened to 'love thine enemy' (Matt 5).

Now God is in the strife,
And I must seek Him there,
Where death outnumbers life,
And fury smites the air.

Men on all sides were fighting, killing each other for God and Country and that didn't make sense. In Siegfried Sassoon's Diaries 1915-1918 he asks:

"The agony of France! The agony of Austria-Hungary and Germany! Are not those equal before God?"

By now he'd served at The Somme, seen men mown down, witnessed the carnage on both sides, lost his brother and a best friend to this war. We see him sometimes tread a fine line between prayer and blasphemy in To Any Dead Officer and again in Attack:

O Christ when will it stop?

O, Jesus make it stop!

Siegfried Sassoon was a good soldier – rather reckless in fact. He was decorated for bravery. Yet Sassoon ended up questioning everything he had been brought up to believe in. This was slaughter on the grand scale, sanctioned by church and state, and he could not reconcile it, and it pained him. Being an officer he dared not speak of this. It would have demoralised the men and he cared deeply about the men. He expresses this frustration in the third stanza of Mystic as a Soldier:

I walk the secret way
With anger in my brain.

That anger eventually burst forth when he published his very open protest in The Times newspaper July 1917 which was subsequently read out in parliament.

"I am making this statement as an act of wilful defiance of military authority, because I believe the war is being deliberately prolonged by those who have the power to end it."

"I have seen and endured the sufferings of the troops, and I can no longer be a party to prolong these sufferings for ends which I believe to be evil and unjust.

I am not protesting against the conduct of the war, but against the political errors and insecurities for which the fighting men are being sacrificed."

Sassoon was aware of the consequences of an officer issuing this statement. True, he had been encouraged in this by Bertrand Russell and the Bloomsbury set but he was not a pacifist and he was no coward. At this point he felt he could no longer be silent and for this he might face court martial and pay the ultimate penalty. His friend and fellow poet, Robert Graves intervened to save his skin, persuading the authorities that Sassoon was suffering from shell shock, and so he was sent to Craiglockhart Castle near Edinburgh for 'treatment' in the hope that, after a period of reflection, he might be persuaded to retract. He was not suffering from shell shock. However in that place he was surrounded by many men who were. Many suffered from severe speech impediments or mutism due to the condition. These were men who, through extreme trauma, had lost the ability to communicate or voice their distress. They literally had been silenced by horror. Their fears had been rendered wordless. It was ironic that Sassoon faced the stark choice, in this setting, to stand by his statement and take the consequences, or to affirm that he was suffering from a mental condition, censor himself and his protest, and return to active service, seemingly cured. It was made clear to him by psychiatrist Dr Rivers, whom he admired, that neither of these courses would be of benefit to the troops on whose behalf he'd lodged the protest. Either way he would be silenced. This and the thought of skipping out of a battle, made him question his own motives.

It was ironic too that it was whilst at Craiglockhart he met Wilfred Owen and they became friends. Sassoon became his mentor and encouraged him in his poetry and in many ways gave us one of the greatest voices of all the war poets. Owen went back to active duty and so did he. Though he still thought it futile, he very much wished to acquit himself well in this war.

Another irony is that it was only through Wilfred Owen that I for one, came to Siegfried Sassoon. How many other voices were silenced forever by that war? We'll never know.

The final line of Mystic as Soldier says:

O music through my clay,
When will you sound again?

'through my clay' has interesting sociological and religious connotations. For many war dead there would be no grave. They were lost in the field. How could they then 'rise again' according to Christian belief? After that war, attitudes towards cremation drastically changed. The logic could not be tolerated that men who fought for their country would be lost forever to God!

Sassoon answers his question at last, in Everyone Sang. He said that the poem 'came to him' and certainly Graves and others didn't regard it as very good poetry, perhaps a little naive. But when a poem 'comes' to a poet, it doesn't just appear out of a blank page and a blank mind. It comes from somewhere deep within and is informed by an evolved sensibility of expression. It is honed by experience. In this case the essence of birdness began in the innocence and birdsong of his Kent childhood (you can trace birds and music through many of his poems) and culminated post war, in this sudden chorus, a release of all the sorrow, joy and passionate anger brought on by such waste of life. It is a poem about making voices heard.

First of all the song lifts his spirits:

I was filled with such delight

As prisoned birds must find in freedom,

Winging wildly

Here were men who longed to fly away, home to their loved ones, away from danger, sickening fear and the horrors of war. They were caught up in a situation they could not escape. Death was a release. The landscape of 'white orchards' like Eden and 'dark fields' Sassoon speaks of is reminiscent of his childhood Kent, but here it emblematic. Heaven was home and the battlefields were darker than Hell. In death this struggle between light and dark is left behind and so in the song, which lifts the spirits of the living and raises the dead. One can almost see a vast host of souls soaring together heavenward:

on - on - and out of sight

still singing.

Everyone's voice was suddenly lifted;

And beauty came like the setting sun:

The military day ends with the bugle call, Sunset also known as Retreat. In the trenches there was little respite, or sleep even at night and Sassoon was known for his night raids. They all longed for rest and the final retreat. When Sassoon writes,

My heart was shaken with tears; and horror

Drifted away ...

despite the punctuation here, as a page poem one sees tears; and horror on the same line and it echoes his 1917 statement: I have seen and endured the sufferings of the troops. For no good reason, they had drifted into war and now seemingly drifted out of it.

Sassoon came from an anglo-catholic and Jewish background. He was familiar with the bird as sacrifice. And when he says:

O, but Everyone

Was a bird;

He truly means 'Everyone' which is why he uses a capital letter. Men on all sides had been sacrificed in, in his opinion, an 'evil and unjust' war and he asks:

"Did Christ not die for these as well?"
the living and the dead, Irish, Scots, Welsh and English, French, Indian, Belgian, Austrian, Hungarian, Polish, German...

and the song was wordless;

of course. Which language would represent them all? How could the dead speak? How could those who'd lost the ability to speak be heard? What language can describe the horrors of that war? Many who served never spoke of it to anyone. Language is wholly inadequate. The song must be wordless. But he says:

the singing will never be done.

I don't think it's just the heavenly choir, Sassoon refers to here though that is certainly there. To sing like a bird also means telling it like it is.

Sassoon had been effectively gagged by the war office in 1917 and now that the war was at an end, he thought the truth would out! History would examine the causes and outcomes of that war. The horror and suffering would be revealed and never be forgotten. He made sure Wilfred Owen was not forgotten. Of course Siegfried Sassoon was delighted that the war was over but he was also eager that Everyone should now be heard so he gave them all a voice in Everyone Sang. Out of the birdness, after all has been swept away, rises this poem, a symbol of peace, a beacon of freedom, a protest against futility. And yes, that war brought about sea-changes in society and in religion but 100 years on, I think there is still little criticism of the conduct of that war, the 'political errors' of which Sassoon wrote, nor acknowledgement of the pity of it. Four years ago a rash of programmes were aired about beginning of WW1 but since then they've all gone quiet. WW11 seems to have taken precedence. Best not to dwell on the futility and carnage, I suspect -- lest we remember. This was a politician's war and had nothing to do with the people who did the fighting and dying but the establishment always closes ranks to maintain power. One will always need people who are prepared to fight.

In November this year all the so called great and good will show up, sombrely attired, at the cenotaph but with no apology on their lips for those who died unnecessarily and brutally one hundred years ago in a cause that was not their own. No anti-war poems will be read. There will be no thought for those who, for the rest of their lives, saw before their waking eyes, the dismembered and dead. Who will bend an ear for the silenced voices? Will there be sorrow for the spinsters and widows made or the unborn of a generation of craftsmen, doctors, artists and poets unmade? No. It will be a celebration of patriotic duty. And

"The old Lie: *Dulce et decorum est*
Pro patria mori"

that Owen and Sassoon and many others so hated, will be perpetuated. The establishment is as it ever was, willing to sacrifice people to its own ends whilst we... we twitter, we tweet but do we sing? Siegfried Sassoon was fond of this poem that 'came to him' in April 1917. He read it out often. It came from a place inside him, deep as death. It sprang from a well of profound and long held melancholy and horror and it sang "through his clay". How could it do otherwise? And if anyone reads it aloud this November, mistaking it for what it is not, it will be because Siegfried Sassoon was a clever man and a great poet and I will smile and say:

Siegfried, this one's for you.

Oonah

I would like to thank James Graham for his helpful comments and input to this editorial.

I found "Siegfried Sassoon A BIOGRAPHY" Max Egremont (2005) Picador: ISBN 978-1-4472-4328-1 very useful in providing background information for this essay.

"No words of mine can soften the blow. There is one consolation for you - your daughter became unconscious immediately after she was hit, and she passed away perfectly peacefully." *-From the letter written by matron Minnie Wood to the parents of staff nurse Nellie Spindler, 1917.*

Women of Passchendaele
Oonah Joslin

For the Passchendaele nurse there was no drill,
no readiness for what she must confront

trying to keep her uniform pristine
negotiating boards from tent to tent

she saw the soldier, half his face blown off,
looked on him as might mother, sister, wife

she dragged him from a shell hole still alive
and gave him sips of water 'til he died

one day she was a surgeon in the field
the next she scribed a diary for the dead

her knees would not stop trembling but her hand
wrote words of consolation to his kin

unconscious moments after the blast
she passed away peacefully at the last

Men of Passchendaele
Oonah Joslin

See, the flood flows under a crazy moon
and warps the planks we laid across the mud.
Eyes loom perpetual, watery in the gloom
beneath the stars amid the smell of blood.

Tree stumps like empty signposts yield
nothing; but stand like sentries at hell's door.
Entrenched, abandoned in the field
our hopes that wars should be no more.

We trample the knowledge that death is unkind.
Life is the next cigarette and a hard won mile.
Impervious now to shellfire, eyes forever blind
meet ours that cannot weep and cannot smile.

Five Australians, members of a field artillery brigade, passing along a duckboard track over mud ...1917
Australia War Memorial

For Anna and John

I am walking this road
to your battlefield
Grandfather
listening to young men's voices flung up
like blackbirds in the wind that flurries them
falling away to a hush:
every step I feel your boot print under mine.

Look! The loch-grey amethyst, given
in that year, 1917, worn in hope of love
flowering into family

if you both were spared:
its promise I carry at my collarbone
as you did, Grandmother.

Pippa Little 2018

Memorial Day

Among these weathered markers, rows
On rows on rows on endless lawn,
My steps disturb a murder of crows
Who bustle awkwardly and are gone.

The echoes of parading drums
Still advertise this warrior trade
To millions more whose martyrdoms
Will follow in their own parade.

The dead get their memorial day,
The color guards and rear guards pass,
While silent stones still stretch away
Across the green and level grass.

Marcus Bales·Monday, 28 May 2018

Illustration for Nikolay Nekrasov poem "Grandfather Mazay and the Hares" by Boris Kustodiev/ Date: 1908/Style: Realism/Genre: illustration

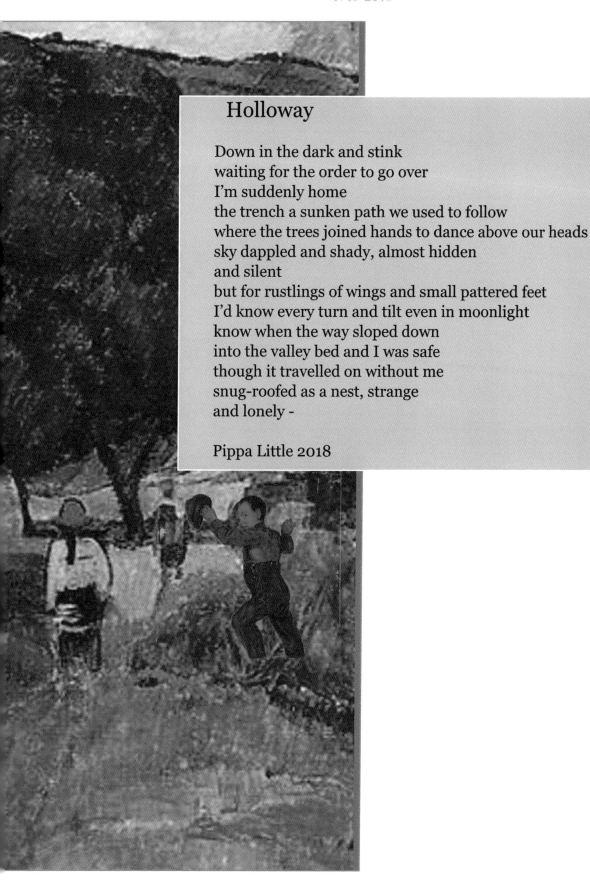

Holloway

Down in the dark and stink
waiting for the order to go over
I'm suddenly home
the trench a sunken path we used to follow
where the trees joined hands to dance above our heads
sky dappled and shady, almost hidden
and silent
but for rustlings of wings and small pattered feet
I'd know every turn and tilt even in moonlight
know when the way sloped down
into the valley bed and I was safe
though it travelled on without me
snug-roofed as a nest, strange
and lonely -

Pippa Little 2018

The Field of Passchendaele by Paul Nash

History of the Great War

Stretcher-bearers found
two dead
one grey one khaki
hand in hand

James Graham.

Previously published by Postcard Poems and Prose

Erinnerung
James Graham

My name is Dieter. I saw my brother Albert die.
His eyes, so like our mother's, were gone.
He fell against the trench-wall, and was still.

there's some corner of a foreign field

My name is Franz. At Langemarck we fought the British.
They were too strong. Our dead were everywhere, their blood
coloured the grass. We could not bury them.

In Flanders fields the poppies blow

My name is Josef. I remember Peter. He was still a child,
just turned fifteen, already smoked a pipe. A shell-burst
tore him in half. It was Kindermord.

They shall grow not old

My name is Bruno. I was at the Somme.
On quiet days we entered the French village,
got some people out. Good folk. We liked them.

We will remember them

Erinnerung – Remembrance
Kindermord – Child murder

ENCYCLOPAEDIA OF MILITARY TERMS
(Continued)

ENGINEERS. -The wise men of the army. They teach the ignorant infantry how to carry sandbags, barbed wire, bath mats, etc., and how to work intricate machinery such as picks and shovels.

ESTAMINET. Translated into English means the " Rendezvous de la Police Militaire." It is where soldiers (including engineers) congregate to spend their unearned increment and to recount the many brave deeds they have done, also to listen to Mademoiselle's "Arf an' Arf" language whilst drinking her "Arf an' Arf" beer.

FORM FOURS. All military experts agree that it is absolutelyimperative that a man be able to form fours before he is fit to defend the Empire. Although this intricate manoeuvre can be accomplished in any number of movements a Drill Instructor usually recommends three. The odd number stands pat, the even numbers step on somebody's toes in the rear with the left foot, and somebody's heel on the right with the right foot. The even number will then find himself viewing the landscape on the back of the odd number's neck, whilst the Empire totters.
Lack of space prevents forming fours in the trenches, but the War Office has the matter under consideration. (From *The Listening Post.}*

Truce

James Graham

'Merry Christmas Tommy!'
'Thanks Fritz, the same to you'.
'Got some lousy grog – here, have a swig'.
'You sound like a Cockney'.

'Cos I am. Me Dad's a barber. Was.
They locked him up. Came over
when I was a nipper. German-English, me.
Or Englisch-Deutsch. *You*
sound like a Cockney – know
the Jolly Farmer's pub in Southgate Road?'

'Gawd blimey! Do I *know* it?
Me uncle has a cobbler's shop next door!'

Oh say it, Tommy.
Say it, Fritz.

If you both live
it may take root.

We've lost our way.

Our common enemies
are in the palaces of Europe.

Based on a true incident reported in a soldier's war diary.
James Graham.

Death Listens by Hugo Simberg/ Date: 1897/Style: Symbolism/Genre: symbolic painting

Sanatorium, St Omer after the Armistice
Tina Cole

Gas light animates our phantom days,
black eyes vague as smoke
close to the shame of this calm
white order where men
are stripped and mummified.

You tell me that the sun
has a dark heart
but that darkness is inside you
erupting through the broken casement
where shells are still falling.

I trace the grid of white tiles seeking
some pattern I can understand,
while bodies are lined up on gravel
you are still snagged on the wire of alarm,
the raw red and black terror
oozing out; time and date irrelevant.

The fug of defeat trapped
between these crowded wards
is like living inside clouded glass
where you breathe gas and smoke
and I must choke on air

so I gather you into my arms
the perfect pieta.

ONCE SCREAMED TO DRUNKS AT THE VETS BAR, MEMORIAL DAY EVENING
TOM SHEEHAN

Sixty-six years now and they come at me, in Chicago, Crown Point, Indiana, by phone from Las Vegas. I tell them how it happened, long after parting, one night when I was in a bar, thinking of them all.

**

Listen, gunmen, all I can smell is the gunpowder on you sharper than booze. You wear your clothes

with a touch of muzzle flash. Is it a story you want...? Listen to the years ago, to the no shooting, to the no rout, to the just dying. The day stank, it wore scabs, had odors to choke tissues and burn secret laminations of the lungs. Rain festered in soot clouds, rose in the Pacific or the Sea of Japan, dumped down on us, came up out of yellow clay like a sore letting out.

The air must have been full of bats, of spider weavings; it was lonely as the lobo, yet a jungle of minds filled it with thought leaves shining with black onyx. Who needs doctors at dying? Prayers sew wounds, piece heads,

hearts, hands together, when blood and clay strike the same irrevocable vein, arterial mush; when God is the earth and clay, silence, the animal taker leaning to grasp.

Listen, gunmen, listen you heroes in mirrors only you see into, we through, it isn't the killing, it's the

ART: PS MLF
Ladies of Arles (Memories of the Garden at Etten) by Vincent van Gogh

dying must be felt, associated, even if it stinks. Blood freezes in hot days of dying, is icicle inside movement of trickery less than glacier's, where a man crawls to his maker up his own veins, is touched, feels the firebrand burn in the cold. Where are the shade trees, cool drinks? Once I froze in the confessional against the fire.

He was a Spick, they said, washed his skin too much, wanted to sandpaper it white, be us, be another man. But we wagered ourselves to get him out of a minefield live as breathing, comrade shot down in the clay in the rain

in the time of bright eyes rolling with thunder's fear. Was it him we carried, or the stone of his monument...?

Tons he was of responsibility, one of us despite the Spick name, man being borne to die.

God is everywhere, the catechism says, my son says, now, years later. It was once a divinity we carried on the poles, with his balls gone pistonless, no more a god to his woman. His image rolled red on the canvas, burned through the handles of the litter as secret as electricity; Spick shooting himself into us, Godhead shooting signs

up shafts of wood.

Lugging God on sticks and canvas is frightening. We felt this. Jesus! We screamed, have You let go of this god? Do You fill him up making him burn our hands? He wanders now for times, rolling himself together, womanless, childless, a journey in dark trees, among leaves, in jungles, to get near You.

God seeking God at the intercept of shrapnel, the tearing down and lifting up by our hands, God in the cement of death. Oh, gunmen, it's the dying not the killing you must speak of. This day is theirs, not ours, belongs to the gods of the dead, of the Spick we carried to his dying and all his brothers, none of them here among us.

Drink, gunmen, one to the Spick and grave's companions, jungle flights they are in to match their god with God.

And think, gunmen, who among us have the longest journey among leaves, in darkness, through the spiders of trees, now.

Soundtrack To Your Exorcism
Jennifer Lothrigel

There were
moaning sounds,
ethereal and dark
with long ommms
made from puckered mouths
and from stillness,
and womb wrapped minds
birthed explosive
Supernovas
from my writhing chest.
Only the brightest stars
become
black holes,
pulled by their own
gravity into nothingness.
I heard the chellist rapidly plucking strings,
her body also shaking in ecstacy.
We all danced through our dark matter,
to sacred songs of deposession.
Our moon lit bodies relieved
of demonic guilt,
ommms became howls,
and the ghosts of forbidden limbs
serenaded our chosen freedom.

Uneme is exorcising the monstrous serpent from the lake by
Utagawa Kuniyoshi/Style: Ukiyo-e/Genre: mythological painting

Mrs Dalloway
Kathleen Thorpe

clarissa, Clarissa,
your beauty and grace
is apparent to all
who look into your face.
When you buy flowers
or when you buy gloves,
do you ever think back
through your life and your loves?

You're famed for the dinners
and parties you hold.
Your life is so simple
even though you were told
that the old Manor House
must be left to the cousin
of the young boy whose death
left a sorrowful chasm.

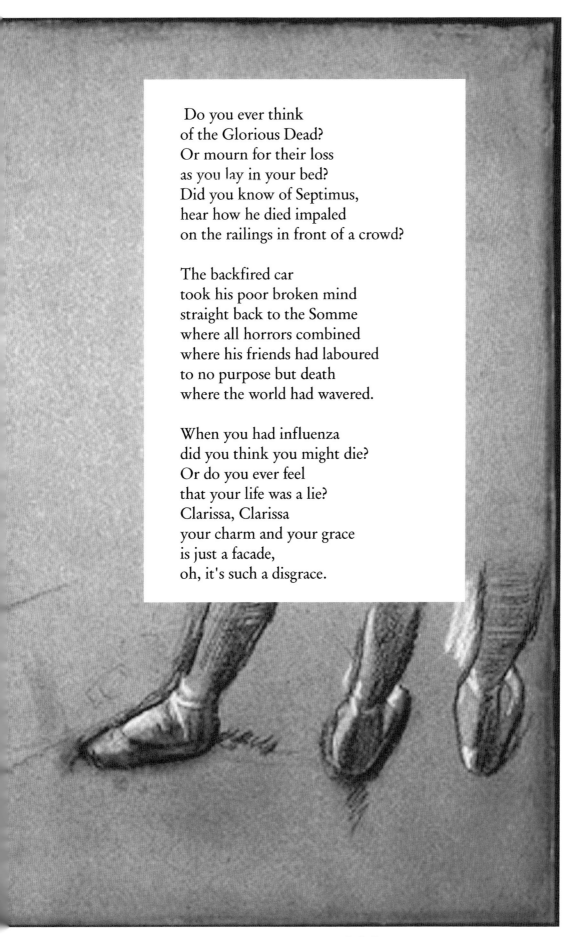

 Do you ever think
of the Glorious Dead?
Or mourn for their loss
as you lay in your bed?
Did you know of Septimus,
hear how he died impaled
on the railings in front of a crowd?

The backfired car
took his poor broken mind
straight back to the Somme
where all horrors combined
where his friends had laboured
to no purpose but death
where the world had wavered.

When you had influenza
did you think you might die?
Or do you ever feel
that your life was a lie?
Clarissa, Clarissa
your charm and your grace
is just a facade,
oh, it's such a disgrace.

Art: Dancer Seen from Behind and 3 Studies of Feet by Edgar Degas

Fair Game
J S Fuller

A track
turned to mud
seeps through the seams
of your best boots

The clanging
from the farm drowns out
a mourning cow's
pain for a lost calf

You trudge
past keeper's field
where young pheasants
try to hide their fear

They run
shell-shocked by muscle
memory that says
'guns, guns, guns'

Recall
another lost breed
fear smothered now
by red poppy shrouds

Cow-like
we voice our lament,
forget they were
bred to be fair game

Woman and child in front of a farm/Piet
Mondrian/ Date: c.1898 - c.1899/ Style:
Impressionism/Genre: portrait

Red & Purple Poppies in the Field
John C. Mannone

I know the name my master gave me.
His owl-whistle call, I'll never forget.
But now, far from home, I only hear
explosions of bombs, rattles of machine
guns. My pupils burn at what I see—
men of England, Germany, falling, I hate
the smell of blood. And their blood runs
the same color in a turbulent hail
of bullets. Shells cutting them in two,
hallowing this blotched ground scarlet.
I am tired of pulling howitzers up hill
and ambulances down. I want to bolt.

All I dream is to plow the turnip fields;
run meadows with grass of golden oats
full of red & purple poppies.
But there're no hallucinations here,
no somnolence for sucklings.
I can no longer whisper in their ears
the senselessness of war, the killing
of my own kind—millions of us—on
all sides. I am in chains that barbwire
my flesh, my ears deafened, eyes blinded
by so many guns—their flash worse than
thunder & lightning, much worse. Where
is whistle call?

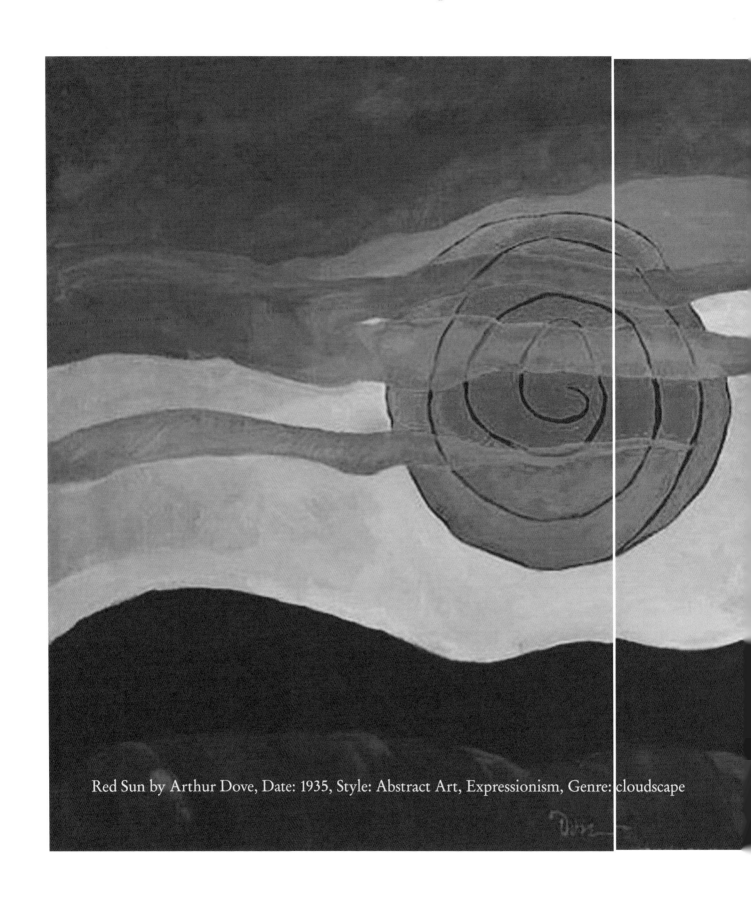

Red Sun by Arthur Dove, Date: 1935, Style: Abstract Art, Expressionism, Genre: cloudscape

In The Silence by John C Mannone

Along the Western Front: Saint-Yvon, Ypres (Belgium)
Christmas Eve 1914

Englishmen and Germans left their trenches, marched
into the woods. They must have heard the Pope pray
that the guns may fall silent...on the night angels sang.
And so they stopped the fighting, stopped the killing.

One remembers *the silence, the eerie sound of silence*
in that *No Man's Land*: trees shattered and strewn;
ground frozen, shelled & bombed leaving a wilderness
to bloom among the tattered scatterings of uniforms.

But a tall pine tree still stood there, where men placed
candles with their waxy light on its boughs. Fatigued
yet hopeful, soldiers exchanged cigarettes and cognac
for black bread and ham; swapped buttons and hats.

Out of the fog, an angel they saw that haloed the treetop,
requested a song. The men knelt, then sang that song,
Silent Night, all the day long and all the night long.
They sang until their throats wore sore

for peace. For a moment, the hissing, cracking, whining
bullets; machine gun fire; and distant voices... all dead
in the silence of the morning. But the mournful cries
of guns filled the valley once again early in the afternoon.

Instruments of Peace by John C Mannone

With the perfect development of the airplane,
wars will be only an incident of past ages

—Orville Wright (1909)

That's what the Wright brothers thought.
Their invention—this heavier than air
machine—would be the great arbiter
of military engagement. No movement
on the ground would go unnoticed by
either army. Instruments of peace.

Wilbur studied doves, killdeer, learned
how they warped their wings to control
their turns and landings light as feathers.

And later, a Frenchman studied insects
to develop the monocoque fuselage—
a single shell, a laminated skin carrying
all the stresses, all the loads, even bombs.

They dragonflied skies in the Great War.
Engines droned, planes buzzed like flies
over the spoils.

Storm Clouds by Arthur Dove

Road in a Winter Garden
by Nikolay Bogdanov-Belsky
/Date: 1920 - 1930/Genre:
 landscape/Media: oil, plywood

PS: MLF Sept, 2018

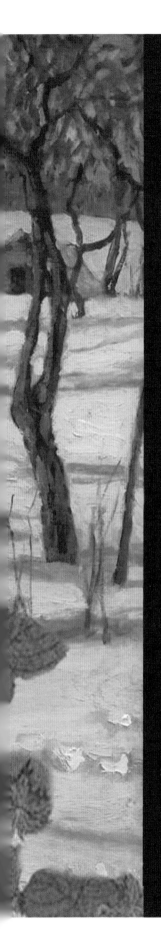

It isn't yet winter
Caroline Hardaker

but all I hold is desiccated bark, retreating to cured origins.
Looking up through heavy roots, stems, wilted ends
I scope the sky; a life ponderous as slate
and prone to cracking at each new quake,
at every thought, sticks fall from their bundle.

All buds have blossomed and dropped,
leaving hollow cups and sham-caskets behind.
Stalks are splinters, tools to pen peculiar notes
woven in marrow odorous with iron-rust,
and which can only be read from the inside, out.

I am a rawhide diary;
my ink's black fading hand-in-hand
with my understanding of its ciphers.
And your face – a folded settlement to live in
between the leaves, a vestige of me, is recorded;
mouth frozen open
in a wide 'O'
of surprise.

A Makeshift Sky
Megan Denese Mealor

no allegory left
in the seeping spoilage
of your ramshackle grin
rusty vibrissa scour
no bee sting promise
for your star-washed cities
or smoking cedar bridges
shuffling the dawn
no bird cherry silk
for these swains of anew
your apologue pallor
blackberry-bleed eyes
bereaving

our retelling, now untold

Sky Blue by Wassily Kandinsky

iced

Two days in January by James Graham

I see from my window
only a slate-grey sky. There is rain
from daybreak until dusk.

My mind is dark today. Hope and humour
are asleep. I cannot say Never mind
to the world's wounded.

The powermen are our affliction.
They make men uniform, obedient, and use them
as bludgeons. Their long arms reach
into the streets, and pluck out one who speaks
forbidden truth. Their busy fingers
shackle the innocent.

I think of Máxima.
Her village in the foothills of Peru
was stolen by a subterfuge the company
calls acquisition. Her people
who have lived there since the Inca times
are dispossessed. Busy men in uniform
have beaten her neighbours. Máxima
has never tired of talking justice; she peeved
the powermen; for living on ancestral land
she was charged with 'land invasion'.

The powermen never read our letters;
lackeys trash our emails. But sometimes
our solidarity heaps up in heavy snowdrifts
against the walls of offices.

There is rain and mourning wind
from dusk till daybreak; I awake
to another weeping sky

but Máxima is free.

I am glad of it.
And over to the East
there's a break in the lowering cloud.
The Sun has not shone through yet.

Perhaps tomorrow.

Cloud Study, Knud Baad, Date: 1850

Reaper
Lesley Timms

Autumn's slanting rays warm contented fingers
Nestling baby onions into soft, receptive earth:
Elemental joy for these season-weathered hands;
Annual comfort for a soul soothed by the cyclical.

But when our unquestioning Rock,
Wheeling eternally on its preordained carousel,
Has whirled through Winter, spun through Spring,
Will I again greet Summer with familiar eyes,
Lulled by self-sedating denial?

Or will Nature's ceaseless cull
Have snatched from close by,
Finally turning my averted face round
To stare death straight in the eye?

While steadfast roots anchor growing bulbs,
Will my once stable world writhe in turmoil;
Blinkered trust in constancy destroyed?

Rain and grieving tears alike will swell these onions.
They'll yield, freely, to Nature's dictate.
Harvested, then ragged holes will pit their ground.
Will deep hollows have been gouged into my heart
By the perennial rhythm of the Reaper?

ELEGY by Tina Cole

You could not hold his life
even though you had been mother,
wife he still slipped the colander
of days, you tried so many ways,
medications, pills, two parts sadness
to one part rage and even then
you could not assuage him
of the dangers that confounded.
You could not hold him.

You could not hold his life
the effort left you breathless
like dashing for a train
only to watch it pull away
the frown of grey carriages
creaking miles to a distant town.
And the pain that left
your voice parched and mute
even one resolute as you.
You could not hold him.

You could not hold his life
when breath was growing short
and death waited in the dawn.
His fading brought only bare walls
into view, another day and so little left
for you. You felt the drain of life,
yet thought and sight remained
vivid, bright, the awful knowing
he might not last another night.
You did not hold him.

You did not hold his life
and when those celebrations
carried joy into Autumn days
there was no pause for you to
stay the sadness
or delay the creeping frost of grief
only relief for those
who returned to go on living
undamaged,
but not whole.

Art: Blind Musician. by Mikhail Nesterov, Date: 1928

Degrees of Silence
Tom Sheehan

Silence comes
out of bullets
that rot in the Earth
or a bucket
of live grenades
some meek hero
threw overboard
in the Leyte Gulf.

Silence is
a wet stone
without a carved name
taking storm knives
in a mile-wide
cemetery in
the Philippines
or bones
in a Kwajalein cave
coming up white as
good teeth
in a hard jaw.

Silence is
a grasped photo,
old black & white,
gone still
in a dead hand,
the smile carried off.

Silence is
a big RBI some kid
drove home in Kansas
in '41 and a father
remembers the ball
going like a bullet
into left center.

Silence is
a brother swimming
100 miles off
a New Zealand beach
saying your name,
through salt
in his teeth,
one last time.

Winter Silence by John Henry Twachtman/Date: 1890 - 1900

Saint Francis in Meditation by Caravaggio, Date: c.1608,Style:
Baroque, Genre: religious painting, Media: oil, canvas

A World Ago
Barry Charman

For Herbert Leo Payne

A world ago
my grandfather slept in the trenches
for two whole days
exhausted as the bullets flew above him
a medic
who'd patched bodies together
but not his own

*

A world ago
another war interrupted
now an air raid warden
keeping others safe
a bomb blew the front door
off his house
and thieves took everything he owned
food
clothes
door
mattress
wedding photos
leaving behind a shell

the very thing
he would never become

13481692R00072

Printed in Great Britain
by Amazon